Pat,

Wishing you few tumbles and good recoveries in your 4th quarter!

Best,

Dennis

4TH QUARTER
FUMBLES

DENNIS STEARNS, CFP®

Stearns Financial Group
Field Guide Series

Put an exclamation point on your life!

4th Quarter Fumbles highlights 25 key fumbles that have the greatest chance of ruining the last quarter of your life. Get ahead of these fumbles and take proactive action! Understanding these fumbles and ways you can prevent them can help you live longer and have a happier, healthier 4th quarter of life.

Praise for *4th Quarter Fumbles: How Successful People Avoid Critical Mistakes Later in Life*

"Dennis Stearns is spot on with Fourth Quarter Fumbles. As a veteran aging services professional, I've seen all too often the missteps in this book. Dennis offers outstanding advice in the book to avoid or alleviate fourth quarter fumbles which all too often leads to crisis."

Stephen Fleming, CEO of Wellspring Life Plan Community, and Chair of Leading Age, the nation's trusted voice for aging and part of the Global Aging Network.

"Dennis has done a marvelous job of challenging each of us to make wise, proactive decisions to maximize our fiscal, physical and mental health as we head into the fourth quarter of life. His concepts are well presented and easy to follow, and many "pearls" will stick with you as you tackle the next three (or four) decades. Implementing these principles may make the fourth quarter the best one yet!"

Dr. Camron Nelson, M.D., Preventative Medicine Physician and President/CEO of the Cooper Clinic in Dallas, Texas. The Cooper Clinic was an early pioneer in disease prevention and is recognized the world over as an authority in wellness, research and education – helping millions lead longer, healthier, happier lives.

Want to learn more about *4th Quarter Fumbles*?

Go to www.FourthQuarterFumbles.com, with 25 additional fumbles to consider. You can take our interactive assessment and get a Fumbleocity™ score with customized ideas on how to avoid future fumbles.

Acknowledgements

How do you prepare for a journey where the winds of fate are predictable but also have many surprises in store for us? Where the winds themselves are blowing harder, allowing us to sail far beyond previous generations and experience wondrous adventures, but also discover hidden rocks and unfamiliar sea monsters that were unknown to our parents or grandparents. How do we prepare for a journey where we can set our own sails to increase our chance of success, or recover from mistakes, filled with both great promise and dangers we haven't prepared for in our life?

A large group of friends, clients and thought leaders in fourth quarter aging best practices helped make this book a reality. I'm grateful for their help, guidance, criticisms and encouragement. They pushed me to strike the right balance between a readable book (early versions resembled *War & Peace*, including 75 fumbles and over 500 pages!) and a helpful reference guide that would provide valuable resources while encouraging readers to up their fourth quarter game.

Thanks to my diverse reader advisory group: Abby D., Bob K., Brent N., Dr. Cam N., Dr. Gary B., Grant F., Haleh M., Janet L., Jed D., Laine and Win D., Lisa L., Mike P., Mitch A., Stephen F., Rob and Janet D., Sherry M., Tim R. and Tom S. Special thanks to Leadership and Legacy's Abby D. who collaborated with me early on to define the many issues that living longer and healthier than previous generations would have for all of us, and refine the thoughts around preparing in the third quarter for what could be for many of us a very long fourth quarter.

And to Dr. C and a number of clients and friends for reinforcing that life is unpredictable and could be shorter *or* longer than we think – a focus on today balanced with an eye towards the future can be one of the most challenging fourth goals.

Thank you to my teammates at Stearns Financial who have been grappling with these issues for over 20 years. There has rarely been one solution to a client's desire to avoid fumbles or recover from actual fumbles. The respectful debates, intense research and always looking for a better path forward have sharpened our skills for the many challenges, financial and non-financial, for our clients that lie ahead.

Thanks to artist and humorist, Harry B., who helped custom design illustrations for each chapter and add a few cartoons to lighten the mood of preparing for perhaps the most challenging, and potentially the most fulfilling, quarter of our life.

Special thanks to my wife Pam, who helped me frame many difficult fourth quarter issues. Her professional experience working with many senior executives preparing (or in many cases, not being prepared!) for the fourth quarter helped in the book chapters and themes. Her stories of late-in-life aging champions as a volunteer and past President of the Board of Hospice of Silicon Valley inspired me to be more optimistic about the opportunity for the slow-go and no-go years to be, on balance, positive. Her own challenging life experiences and adaptive decisions with aging friends and family are reflected in this book.

My own goal is to be a lifelong learner and doer in the quest for a spectacular fourth quarter!

Forward

by Mitch Anthony,
Fourth Quarter Jedi Expert

What is the point of building a nest-egg, only to put it in a dying tree? For the past two decades I've studied the lifestyles of those who retire and have seen this regrettable phenomenon. Some people retire well, and some people don't. Those who retire well first figure out how to invest in themselves and then their money. They make lifestyle choices that are edifying and not destructive. They protect their greatest assets—the life-long relationships that have brought them this far. They listen to good advice and exercise discipline when the world looks like it's going mad.

Those who don't retire well follow an altogether different course. They don't look for places to exercise their gifts and aptitudes. They become bored, grumpy and surly. They allow bad habits to fester and grow. Worst of all, their attitude gets poisoned with self-pity, aimlessness, and disenchantment—eroding the most valuable relationships in their life. If compounding wealth is, as Ben Franklin described it, the eighth wonder of the world, then gray divorce (splitting up later in life) is the eighth blunder, especially when it happens later in life. I define divorce (mathematically) as the exact opposite of compounding wealth.

Dennis has hit the bullseye with Fourth Quarter Fumbles. The worst feature of those I've observed who do not retire well is that they lose their curiosity and coach-ability and stop listening to the people they should be listening to. The result is a complete erosion of everything they have gathered and built, finances notwithstanding.

If we were to take a little seed when we were young, and then work that seed into a tree, and that tree over decades into an orchard, how vigilantly would we watch that orchard? Unfortunately, far too many people make lifestyle and financial decisions in their later years that literally burn down the orchard. But, it need not be so.

Dennis has spent a lifetime helping people make better informed financial decisions. He has cared for their well-being and given time-tested advice to help them grow their wealth and avoid fumbles. Imagine the frustration of helping people for 30+ years get to this point—only to see some of them start fumbling it away in the "red zone" of life in their retirement years. Now, you understand why Dennis wrote this book.

When I was younger, I had the naïve idea that people always became wiser as they grew older. That balloon got popped early in my journey as I watched so many mature people I knew move toward calcification and intractability rather than an openness and willingness to listen to wisdom for their situation.

Financial mistakes made later in life can and do have much more dire and irreconcilable consequences because the mature person doesn't have another lifetime, or sufficient opportunity, to replenish what has been lost. None of us wants to see a lifetime of gathering blown away by a cyclone of impetuous irrationality, and it is wise financial advice that will prevent such an occurrence.

Dennis is a well-respected financial planner and has been nationally recognized as such. He's not looking to sell a financial product or idea; he's seeking to help people make wise financial decisions. He knows full well that it is better to prepare than to repair. This book is preparation and sage warning against the later-in-life, self-sabotaging opportunities that await us all—if we're not aware.

Dennis is also an astute and compassionate observer. He has seen the patterns and the igniting behaviors and mindsets that set them into motion. He knows how to help people avoid the fumbles that erase all the yardage gained in life. He cares enough to tell the truth—and the real-life stories that so poignantly illustrate these truths.

Retirement years, if one has sufficient assets, can and should be the most rewarding and significant years of our lives. We have the freedom we've always desired, the autonomy to pursue our bucket list of places, people and pursuits—and hopefully, the health to follow through on those desires. We need not make the mistakes that Dennis writes about, but we all have the potential to do so. Read this book and circle the chapter titles that remind you of your inclinations or circumstances. If you ever find yourself losing your grip on the situation, go back and read that chapter again.

Let's finish this journey the best way possible…with both hands raised in the air.

Mitch Anthony, Author, *The New Retirementality*

Table of Contents

Introduction

fumble

[fuhm-b*uh* l]

verb (used without object), **fumbled, fumbling.**

1. to feel or grope about clumsily:
    She fumbled in her purse for the keys.

2. *Sports.* to fumble the ball.

verb (used with object), **fumbled, fumbling.**

3. to make, handle, etc., clumsily or inefficiently:
    to fumble an attempt; He fumbled his way through the crowded room.

4. *Sports.* to fail to hold or maintain hold on (a
    ball) after having touched it or carried it.

noun the act of fumbling:

5. *We completed the difficult experiment* without a fumble.

6. Sports. an act or instance of fumbling the ball.

Synonyms
bungle, botch, mishandle, spoil, muff.

We all make fumbles during our lives. Some are small, like backing into a car in a parking lot. Some are big and create consequences for us and those we love for the rest of our lives. This book is about the big fumbles we can make in the fourth quarter of our lives and how to avoid them – or if we make them, how to minimize their damage and bounce back.

Helping clients avoid fumbles, or helping them recover from them, has been a key part of my work in the past three decades. I began to notice that some very savvy clients, people I respected and looked up to, entered the later stages of life and struggled. They may have done extensive financial and investment planning but then encountered non-financial challenges that, surprisingly, they weren't prepared to deal with and that created major fumbles. Make too many fumbles, financial or nonfinancial, and a life well lived can become very difficult.

I also noticed that many clients and friends flourished in the fourth quarter. They found ways to avoid the fumbles. What's more, they found ways to accomplish positive goals that they once thought would be unattained. They had fun! Even when life dealt them some bad cards, they bounced back to experiencing even more fun experiences with family and friends.

Working with many couples and singles, I've seen differences in how they deal with avoiding fumbles and bouncing back from them. Whenever I use the term *life partner*, if you don't currently have one, consider the reference to your best friend in life, someone who will give you good advice and the unvarnished truth no matter what.

Each chapter of this book deals with ways to avoid fumbles as well as action steps that can lead to a more successful fourth quarter. The twenty-five "red-zone" fumbles are the ones my colleagues and I have encountered more frequently or that have had a greater impact on a successful fourth quarter – as compared with an average fumble.

Each chapter mentions additional fumbles that you can review on the www.FourthQuarterFumbles.com website.

This book ends with a number of tools and resources in the Appendices – additional resources for those who want to study "best practices" for the fourth quarter. The Resources section contains many of my favorite books on aging out of the hundreds I've read. If you find that you're weaker in one or two areas than the others, this will give you a quick guide to how to sharpen your skills through additional study.

Also included in the Appendix is a self-directed "Assessment Survey." Whether you decide to take the survey before or after reading this book, it can help pinpoint blind spots and areas that need more attention. This survey is also available in digital form with instant scoring of your Fumbleocity™, your likelihood of experiencing fumbles, at www.FourthQuarterFumbles.com.

CHAPTER 1

Why So Many Seniors Fumble the Ball in the Fourth Quarter

A 2016 study by the Employee Benefit Research Institute (EBRI) ana-lyzed retirement satisfaction trends between 1998 and 2012. Almost 12% of retirees had switched from "very satisfied" to "moderately satis-fied," and many people declined to "not at all satisfied." This happened in the highest asset quartile as well as lower quartiles. Why are people at the same financial circumstances and stage of the fourth quarter of their life declining in satisfaction levels from the late 1990s to current times?

Perhaps the greatest question is how could this be happening at the same time that people entering the fourth quarter believe they will live longer, at more healthy levels, and have more recreational opportunities than any generation in the history of humankind?

There are many explanations for the odd decline in satisfaction levels in the fourth quarter. The best one is that we haven't been prepared by our parents, mentors, or society for an extended last chapter of life. It's a relatively new phenomenon that contains many opportunities, as well as numerous potential pitfalls, that previous generations never had to consider.

Windmills of Your Mind

"Keys that jingle in your pocket,
Words that jangle in your head,
Why did summer go so quickly?
Was it something that you said?

Lovers walk along a shore,
And leave their footprints in the sand,
Is the sound of distant drumming
Just the fingers of your hand?

Pictures hanging in a hallway
And the fragment of a song,
Half-remembered names and faces
But to whom do they belong?

When you knew that it was over
You were suddenly aware
That the autumn leaves were turning
To the color of her hair.

Like a circle in a spiral,
Like a wheel within a wheel,

Never ending or beginning
On an ever-spinning reel
As the images unwind
Like the circles that you find,
In the windmills of your mind."

I have worked with hundreds of clients and conducted interviews with dozens of people who were approaching, or had already entered, the fourth quarter of their lives. Like the singer of this Oscar-winning song from the 1960s, many of them expressed misgivings. Typically, such people have spent their entire lives trying to make good decisions – learning from mistakes, adjusting when they sensed danger or opportunity, and prospering along the way. They want their remaining time to be happy and productive, but a common refrain has been that they are suddenly in unfamiliar territory. What should they focus on? Their golf or tennis game? Family? Health? Hobbies? A bucket list?

And that is not the end of questions that flood over them. For those who have prepared well financially and emotionally for the fourth quarter, what would cause a dramatic turnaround in fortunes? Given healthcare advances and longevity trends, how long could this fourth quarter last? Could it go into overtime? If they have a life partner, a common concern is whether their partner will be a helpmate or an anchor. Will their life partner be an asset near-term but a liability longer term?

The singles that I have interviewed share many of the same concerns that couples have, and they have additional concerns about entering this phase alone. They want to know what special risks lie ahead. Some singles shared that they jumped into relationships that they shouldn't have just to hedge the risks of growing old. A few believed that this could be the first of many fumbles they would make but felt trapped and unable to adjust as they had earlier in life. After all, who gets divorced after age 65? Turns out, "gray divorce," is sadly one of the fastest growing trends today.

Fortune favors the prepared, and few people prepare for the fourth quarter as they did for their career, family, and other major life events. Past generations didn't need to prepare: The fourth quarter was often shorter than previous ones.

In the recent past, just 20 to 30 years ago, one spouse typically became chronically ill within 7 to 10 years after retirement (it was typically the husband) and the other spouse became the caregiver. One would usually die by age 70 or 75, and the other would be so worn out with caregiving roles that he or she wouldn't last too much longer. This scenario still happens, of course, but for many people the good years now stretch out longer and there are more opportunities to spend money, help struggling children, and provide gifts or travel experiences for grandchildren.

The fourth quarter can be stressful. Over half of the top-20 stress indicators, positive and negative, in the Holmes-Rahe Life Stress inventory (see Appendix 7) happen in various stages of the fourth quarter. If you retire, have stress with money, have a new grandchild, and have major changes in several life activities (like recreation) all in one year, the Holmes-Rahe model says you have a 50% chance of a major health breakdown in the next two years!

Some of the stress reflected in the EBRI study can also be attributed to more challenging financial conditions during this time frame, including two very difficult recessions. It's also likely that these changes in satisfaction levels can be traced to the media relentlessly highlighting the worst of everything happening all around the world, repeating the stories incessantly, giving the impression that the entire world is on the verge of collapse.

A realization that the fourth quarter of our lives may last longer than we thought is causing more stress in those who didn't prepare well. Much of the declining satisfaction levels are related to the feelings of people receiving pensions versus those managing their own retirement plans: 57.5% of pension recipients were "very satisfied" after 15 years of retirement in the EBRI study as compared to only 46.5% of people without a pension.

Many thought leaders in the healthy aging space that I interviewed think the issues outlined in this book will cause the "very satisfied" numbers above to decline further, even for the ones with no financial worries.

Loss of Community

For thousands of years, the norm was that elders helped teach young people by telling stories of their experiences. People grew up and rarely ventured more than a walk or horseback ride from their villages. The elders helped give the younger members of the family perspective on what they needed to learn to advance to the next stage of life. When the elders got to the later years of their lives, the younger generation would care for them, usually in their own homes.

This "community" approach to the fourth quarter has shattered in America and in many places around the world. Enhanced mobility and globalization are partially responsible, along with new learning tools for a new techno-information age that lead many members of the younger generation to have less respect for the wisdom of their elders.

Ironically, demographic experts believe the Millennial generation has, on average, a 5- to 7-year setback from previous generations in their emotional intelligence (EQ). Although many of them are "smart" by IQ standards, they are not as smart when it comes to recognizing that what they don't know can hurt them in their careers and in the development of personal relationships. In the past, elders helped the younger generations learn EQ along with IQ.

Add into that the effects of a world moving faster than at any time in history: McKinsey says the current techno-industrial revolution dwarfs earlier industrial revolutions, with the current revolution being much more impactful, moving at ten times the speed of the first industrial revolution and having three hundred times the power! This puts pressure on everything from government policy-making, to economic competition, to pressures on the younger generation to be faster, better, and stronger.

The loss of community we are experiencing is a potential cultural disaster that is just starting, only decades in the making. Society is trying to adjust to all of these dramatic changes, including the new role of elders, but it's an increasingly difficult process of adjustment for young and old alike. It also creates more ways that people can fumble.

I'm often asked to identify the top things to focus on in the fourth quarter to avoid fumbles. Because I'm a professional financial planner, most think I'll say, "*How much?*" – meaning what's the amount of money needed to enjoy a comfortable fourth quarter of life. Although having enough money has been one of several key focus areas of my long career and is certainly important for many people, there are many more fumbles to worry about than just money.

If you can figure out your *Why?* (your purpose in the next chapter of your life), your *Who?* (the people that you will hang out with most of the time), and eventually your *Where?* (the places that you will live at various stages of the fourth quarter), you'll lower the chance of major fumbles. Tying all of these together is the *How?* – how you make decisions and take action in each of these areas often separates the average fourth quarter experience from the spectacular one. A groundbreaking 1988 MacArthur study on aging found high correlations among all of these factors, which can both build on each other positively to create successful aging and detract from each other negatively to create a multitude of fourth quarter fumbles.

If you have enough money but don't know your *Why?*, *Who?*, and *Where?*, and the *How?* of implementing each area well, chances are the ensuing fumbles will increase your expenses, and possibly destabilize an otherwise sound financial plan, especially in the health-care area.

Three very specific areas highly impact your ability to answer the *Why*, *Who*, *Where* and *How* questions throughout the fourth quarter: making better decisions, maintaining wellness and mobility, and having resiliency.

First, making better decisions applies to every aspect of dealing with issues in life, especially in the fourth quarter. You will have to decide what to do about important issues: "What is my financial plan?" "How am I going to spend more free time than I've ever had?" "How can I keep myself interested and interesting as I get older?" These are critical to how happy you're going to be as the fourth quarter evolves. Even if you have a poor track record for decision-making, you can do better. I've outlined some ideas in chapter 3 to help you make better fourth quarter decisions.

Second, maintaining wellness and mobility of mind and body is important for general health and happiness in the fourth quarter. Our health is our number-one asset and should be treated accordingly. We should strive for wellness, which is a level of health well beyond not having any illnesses. The excellent book *Younger Next Year: Live Strong, Fit, and Sexy – Until You're 80 and Beyond* by Chris Crowley and Henry S. Lodge cites many examples where taking fitness and mobility more seriously in the fourth quarter can add years to your life and life to your years.

Third, having resiliency, the ability to bounce back from a fumble, is vital to fourth quarter success because even the best life plans encounter fumbles. Self-confidence can be tested or shattered as we face serious illnesses, lose loved ones, or endure other extreme experiences. We can adapt and grow if we have a good support system around us.

The great news is these three critical areas can all be improved and sharpened with purposeful efforts even as aging attempts to dull their edge and throw you off your game.

Live Long and Prosper?

Fourth quarter fumbles are happening more and more frequently as lifespans increase and quality of life improves. Modern medicine is constantly progressing in its ability to help us when our bodies start to decline as we age. Stearns Financial has been assisting many of our clients with the transition into and through the three stages of the fourth quarter. The reason for this book is that we see clients, friends, and relatives encounter dangers and landmines they never dreamed possible. They often knew some of the risks but couldn't avoid them for a variety of reasons.

Lifespans have been increasing in our generation despite some setbacks to longevity as a result of the current obesity epidemic in the U.S. Today, the average 65-year-old in the U.S. has a 20-year life expectancy. But the averages don't tell the whole story. One out of every four 65-year-olds today will live past age 90, and one out of ten will live past age 95.

Considering that medical advances are occurring at an ever-increasing rate, many longevity experts and scientists predict that lifespans will increase by at least 10 years by 2025! The even better news is that many people in the fourth quarter of their lives are already enjoying a higher quality of life than the previous generation. This trend is also expected to expand by 2025, suggesting more good years ahead.

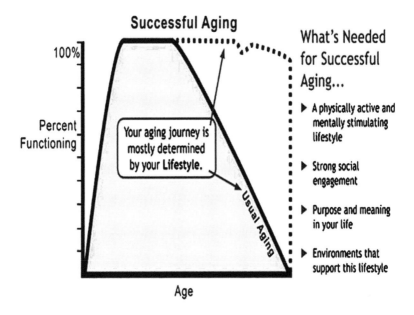

The above chart, which was presented at a major conference on aging, shows the "usual trend" of aging versus "successful aging," where a health event causes a temporary blip down in quality of life. Good medical treatment and good lifestyle choices then allow many individuals to push the "high quality, longer life" limits out further than previous generations could.

One challenge of this expanding trend is that most people set aside enough money to live comfortably to age 85 or 90, not expecting they would need to stretch their money out longer. Another challenge is that spouses or life partners come into the fourth quarter at different preparation levels and they often age at different paces. They also haven't considered what it takes to stay engaged with life this long and keep a marriage together. The acceleration of these aging trends creates many more questions about the future than answers, and I will do my best to provide ideas on better preparation while also providing insight into other fourth quarter areas that will be trickier to navigate going forward.

The Three Stages of the Fourth Quarter

Most people go through three stages during the fourth quarter of their lives. These have been described by author Michael Stein. The first, which he terms the *go-go stage*, usually lasts 10 to 15 years. If people "retired" at age 65, they stay in this stage through age 75 or 80, and they tend to be fairly active and mobile, continue to travel, pursue hobbies, and be engaged with life.

There are a number of transition risks in moving from the third quarter of our lives to stage 1 of the fourth quarter (the go-go years, usually ages 65 to 80);

- Trouble adjusting to numerous fourth quarter lifestyle changes
- One life partner still working full time
- Lack of a good transition plan
- Spending problems as a result of too much free time
- Boredom leading to depression and bad financial or life choices
- Inadequate exercise program

Many retirees experience some fumbles in stage 1, but most of the risk is actions or inactions that set the stage for multiple fumbles in stage 2.

Transition risks for going from the stage 1 (go-go years) to stage 2 (slow-go years, usually ages 75 to 85) include the following:

- Not ready emotionally to deal with slow-go stage
- Declining exercise program
- One life partner is still in go-go stage
- Shrinking social network
- No health-care advocate or a weak advocate

Stage 2 of the fourth quarter is when you begin to slow down a bit (also called *slow-go*), doing fewer of the things you enjoy. This stage usually lasts for 7 to 12 years, sometimes more if you're fit and have good genes; this is much longer than previous generations enjoyed, and that's both good and bad news. You have a longer life to travel and experience the "encore" effect, doing something you love (with or without money) that you didn't have the time or resources to do in your working life. However, body parts begin to break down more frequently. As one of our young-at-heart 80-something clients likes to say, this is the stage when it takes as much time repairing your body as it does repairing your home.

Transition risks for going from stage 2 (slow-go) to stage 3 (no-go years, usually ages 85 to 90+) include the following:

- Life partner unprepared for caregiving tasks
- Lack of good caregivers for singles
- Insufficient mobility or exercise program
- Not eligible for acceptance into a continuing-care retirement community
- Elder abuse
- Lack of organization is magnified

Stage 3 is the last few years of your life where it is clear things are winding down. This is also called the *no-go stage*. In this stage, the struggle is with loss of control and searching for meaning in the decisions and events of our life. Whether it's stated directly or not, most people in this stage are facing enormous self-inflicted pressure to make sense of their current situation. If they can develop better skills earlier, and better connections with their family and friends, they stand a much better chance of being a wise sage versus a grumpy old person.

Adding to the complex landscape, somewhere in the slow-go stage, some people develop a form of dementia or Alzheimer's (or another debilitating disease) that pushes them more rapidly into the no-go stage. The chart below, from a study conducted by the American Geriatric

Society, shows a major loss of financial ability (the solid line) in the 5 years *preceding* the diagnosis of dementia, with less of a decline in those 5 years in other areas (the dotted line). The conclusion?

Many financial fumbles can occur when everyone believes the elder still has control of most of their faculties.

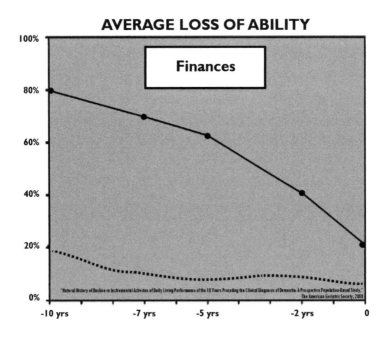

The no-go years can be especially difficult to handle for those who don't have a strong spiritual center. We have seen it test even devout members of the clergy. This stage has a different set of fumbles to be wary of, with poor decisions in earlier stages or unfortunate life circumstances making some fumbles unavoidable at this time.

With a much longer fourth quarter in the cards for some people, it provides many more opportunities to explore their *Why?, Who?, Where?* and *How?,* and do what they've always wanted to do.

An extended fourth quarter (ideally going into "overtime") also provides more chances to make mistakes in areas that parents or grandparents never had to worry about.

Jim and Carolyn's Story

Here is a real-life case study that brings home many of the challenges we all face in the fourth quarter of our lives. The names and context have been changed to protect privacy.

Jim and Carolyn reached their golden years with what appeared to be more than enough money in investments and a good, balanced approach to spending, with children who were reasonably self-sufficient. Most financial planners would have given them an "A" rating and predicted a fantastic, enjoyable retirement. Then a series of fumbles began that culminated in an outcome they thought they had avoided.

Jim's fourth quarter balance wheel looked like this at his retirement:

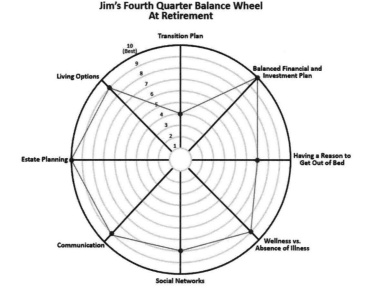

Jim's Fourth Quarter Balance Wheel
At Retirement

1. Transition Plan – 4.

2. Balanced Financial and Investment Plan – 10.

3. Having a Reason to Get Out of Bed – 7.

4. Wellness versus Absence of Illness – 9.

5. Social Networks – 8.

6. Communication – 9.

7. Estate Planning – 10.

8. Living Options – 9.

Carolyn's fourth quarter balance wheel looked like this at Jim's retirement:

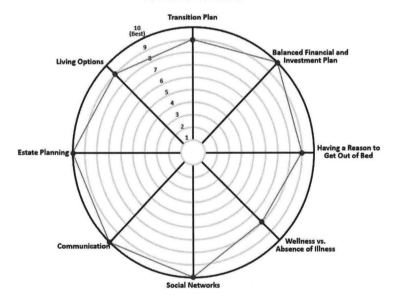

Carolyn's Fourth Quarter Balance Wheel At Jim's Retirement

1. Transition Plan – 9.

2. Balanced Financial and Investment Plan – 10.

3. Having a Reason to Get Out of Bed – 9.

4. Wellness Versus Absence of Illness – 8

5. Social Networks – 10.

6. Communication – 10.

7. Estate Planning – 10.

8. Living Options – 9.

Note: In Appendix 6, there is a blank wheel and instructions on how to complete your own Fourth Quarter Balance Wheel.

The first fumble: Jim became bored. In his previous job as a well-respected executive he had a team that looked up to him, trusted him, and went the extra mile. Jim was part of forward-looking planning that included a sharp management team getting research from equally sharp consultants. When he retired he did it cold turkey. One week he was in the middle of smart people making important decisions, and the next week he was trying to figure out how to fill in the big gaps of time between golf games and dinner with his wife.

Carolyn was a nurse, enjoyed her job and the people she worked with, and decided to retire at the same time Jim did so they could play together. Unfortunately, Jim's idea of playing and Carolyn's vision of ideal didn't line up most of the time.

Jim didn't know it, but within several years he was slipping into a mild form of depression. His regular exercise routine faltered. He began to eat more and saw his weight climb. He disconnected more from his friends, family, and Carolyn. Clothes didn't fit quite right, so he wanted to socialize less. His hearing was faltering and he didn't like the way his new hearing aid filtered background noises in restaurants. His new life didn't feel satisfying.

The second fumble: A financial crisis arrived. Jim was already on edge and reading too many scary Internet articles on the potential for the financial crisis to become another decade-long depression. He sold stocks near their lows and moved to cash. Several weeks later, he called his financial advisor (not SFG at the time!) and asked his opinion. His advisor wasn't like the consultants he had worked with in business: He told him the future was uncertain and first suggested that Jim and Carolyn should ride out the storm. Then the advisor's tone changed a few weeks later and he admitted that this was an unusual time and that he didn't really have a good plan to suggest. Unnerved, Jim moved even more money to cash without consulting Carolyn.

Carolyn would later say she trusted Jim but should have been more engaged in decision-making. She feels it was more her fault than Jim's; he offered to include her in discussions but she wasn't really as interested in the finances and was focused on grandchildren and travel.

The third fumble: The original plan had been to downsize their home when they were deeper into retirement, perhaps 10 to 15 years out. Now they had less money than when they retired and Jim's anxiety day in and day out was wearing on Carolyn. They decided to downsize sooner, selling their home in a down market for less than it was really worth. It depressed Jim more. His history of buying and selling homes at an ever-increasing profit had just been broken. Carolyn became concerned that they were making knee-jerk decisions and wanted to be involved more. Her confidence in the future and Jim's decision-making ability declined.

The fourth fumble: Jim and Carolyn's youngest child, Emily, had graduated from college and couldn't find a good job that fit her training and interests. The financial crisis had made it even tougher. She came to dad for advice but he was not the same confident businessman who had helped her so many times before. He was anxious, and that made her even more fearful. Emily did what she had always done when she was stressed out – she spent money. First, she splurged on electronic gadgets, then on clothes, then on trips. She ran up a $20,000 credit-card bill and came to her parents for help. Both parents were shocked that their youngest daughter, who normally had good common sense, had dug a deep financial hole for herself.

Jim and Carolyn argued daily about the best course of action. They had had a few arguments in their life about what was best for the children, but this time was different. The stress of other parts of their life was spilling over into the discussion about Emily. They felt as if Emily should stand on her own two feet, but they also didn't want her ruining her credit so early in her life or even declaring bankruptcy if she couldn't get her financial life in order. Now that their own financial life was less certain, they weren't even sure they could help Emily without harming their own financial future. Their relationship with Emily became strained over a period of several months.

The fifth fumble: Jim started having more severe health problems. It was likely related to his increased levels of stress, lower level of exercise, and poor eating habits. First it was elevated cholesterol levels. Then it was high blood pressure. Jim's doctor wanted him to be on anti-depressants but Jim thought that would be admitting he was in a place he never wanted to be. Several prescriptions later, Jim started having unusual side effects. Jim's doctor couldn't isolate the problem. Several other specialists they consulted had conflicting recommendations.

Jim's medical problems affected his attitude about life, and he couldn't travel as much with Carolyn to spend time with the grandchildren. He became increasingly irritable and downright grumpy. He had trouble balancing his checkbook at times and let a key insurance policy lapse.

The sixth fumble: Carolyn finally had enough of Jim's poor attitude and increasingly erratic behavior. After multiple attempts to get him to a new doctor or to counseling, she suggested marital counseling. He refused. At age 70 and in good health, looking at another 10, maybe even 20, strong years ahead of her, Carolyn decided a trial separation was needed. Some of the kids understood, others thought she needed to be there for dad. Carolyn filed for divorce at age 72.

The seventh fumble: Having two households put additional strain on the family budget. Carolyn had to severely curtail her spending and forgo many of the trips with grandchildren and friends that she was looking forward to when Jim retired.

Jim become more and more isolated from his friends and family, began spending money erratically, and slowly diminished his own net worth.

In only 10 years, Jim and Carolyn's fourth quarter wheels looked very different:

Jim's fourth quarter balance wheel at age 75 looked like this:

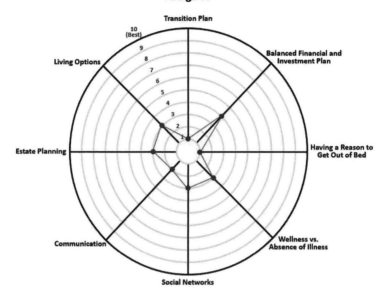

**Jim's Fourth Quarter Balance Wheel
At Age 75**

1. Transition Plan – 1 (Jim withdrew from life).

2. Balanced Financial and Investment Plan – 4 (Poor decisions and split household created tremendous financial pressure).

3. Having a Reason to Get Out of Bed – 1 (Jim felt like he had little purpose in his life despite intervention attempts by his son).

4. Wellness Versus Absence of Illness – 3 (Jim's health was declining and he didn't do anything proactively to reduce the decline).

5. Social Networks – 3 (Jim was anxious and angry a lot, and his family and many of his friends didn't want to be with him as much).

6. Communication – 2 (Jim's great communication skills declined rapidly and were affected by his "glass is mostly empty" mind-set).

7. Estate Planning – 3 (Jim's back-up attorneys in fact, his ex-wife and son, now didn't want to serve in this capacity for him).

8. Living Options – 3 (Jim decided to age in place in a small home).

Carolyn's fourth quarter balance wheel at her age 75 looked like this:

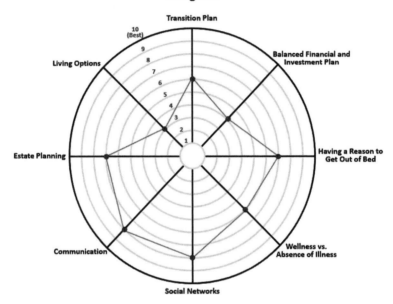

Carolyn's Fourth Quarter Balance Wheel At Age 75

1. Transition Plan – 6 (Carolyn's transition plan was now much more uncertain, focused primarily on her family).

2. Balanced Financial and Investment plan – 4 (Poor decisions and split household created tremendous financial pressure).

3. Having a Reason to Get Out of Bed – 7 (Grandchildren became a primary focus).

4. Wellness Versus Absence of Illness – 6 (Carolyn had some light depression and a growing lack of

mobility after her dream of how the fourth quarter would turn out was shattered, which made her less interested in exercise and eating well).

5. Social Networks – 8 (Most of her married friends stopped calling for dinner dates now that she was by herself).

6. Communication – 8 (Carolyn still had a pretty good communication tree with true friends and family).

7. Estate Planning – 7 (Most of her plans for late in stage 3 of the fourth quarter were still intact).

8. Living Options – 3 (Carolyn's ideal retirement community was now out of reach financially).

The eighth fumble: Jim developed early dementia signs at age 75. At first, everyone including his doctors thought it was just normal senior issues associated with getting older. In the next 3 years, Jim became more and more difficult to be around and he withdrew from life with very little contact with family or friends. He became convinced he would win the Publisher's Clearing House sweepstakes and ordered tens of thousands of dollars of merchandise, which sat stacked in his living room, most still in unopened boxes.

The children finally were able to get the power of attorney enforced and Jim was placed in an Alzheimer's-care unit. His quality of life was miserable, and he never quite understood what had happened to most of his friends; who now infrequently visited. Jim died at age 80, depressed and virtually penniless.

Jim didn't do well at answering the questions of *Why* he existed beyond work and *Who* to hang around with to help him stay balanced.

Carolyn did better, dealing with Jim's fumbles that upended her own fourth quarter journey. She is getting her life somewhat back on track, including a gentleman companion she met in her eighties who helped her heal and have a better late-stage fourth quarter.

This cautionary tale is unfortunately true. Some of the events and decisions made by Jim and Carolyn were unavoidable, but many of the problems they encountered, and resulting fumbles, were avoidable. They could have adjusted and bounced back better as each challenge tested them.

Working with their children today, it's interesting that they view Jim's fourth quarter fumbles as a cautionary tale for future generations. Knowing Jim as I did, I think he would have preferred to have been a more positive role model for healthy aging. His earlier self would have at least been somewhat happy that his family was learning important lessons for the future, just not in the "avoid what Jim did" way things turned out.

The Set of the Sails

by Ella Wheeler Wilcox

One ship drives east, and another west
With the self-same winds that blow;
'Tis the set of the sails
And not the gales
That decides the way to go.

Like the winds of the sea are the ways of fate,
As we voyage along through life;
'Tis the will of the soul
That decides its goal,
And not the calm or the strife.

The Example of Elaine

Here are some more real-life issues to consider from a model of successful aging. Elaine in Colorado, who believes her fourth quarter started later than most, intends to make her "overtime" as good for her and her family and friends as possible.

No matter how fit you are, sometime between 75 and 80 you will be entering your fourth quarter of life. I believe it is a mistake to not recognize this. Most all of us go through life with at least a few deferred activities ("Someday I'm going to . . ."). It is important to recognize when someday has arrived and you say to yourself, "If not now, when?"

The game of football is run by the clock, and each quarter has an equal amount of time. The game of life is not like that. Time goes faster the older you get: Ask any older person. I don't care how much you plan and educate yourself; the fourth quarter sneaks up on you and you wind up saying, "Where did the years go and how did I get to be this old?" Many of us then console ourselves by remembering what a wonderful life we have had thus far, etc., etc. That said, we are still a little bit in shock when we own up to the fact that we have only a limited number of years left.

Then there is the physical decline. One can eat right, exercise your rear end off (literally), and read all the books on "growing younger," etc. You are still going to get older (if you are lucky), and you are not going to be able to do at 70 what you could do at 60, or at 80 what you could do at 70. You can stretch this time frame some, but not forever. I expect I will be shocked when I (hopefully) reach 90 and realize my physical limitations. I'm not even going to mention mental decline as that is a whole other subject.

I cannot stress enough how important it is to fully understand the insidious changes that sneak up on you as you age. I once thought if I hiked up Mt Whitney every year I would never lose my ability to do it. I did it twice, but not again in this lifetime. I have friends even younger than me who used to love to travel to Europe who now say they no longer have the desire. I expect my day will come. When the day comes, it's fine; we all have other things that bring us joy. What is really important and is the point of my comments is this: Don't put off doing things you want to do, thinking you will still be able and interested in doing them later.

The fourth quarter is by far the most difficult from my point of view, and probably only those of us experiencing it can fully understand just how challenging it is. Gone is someday. It's all about now with the realization that tomorrow might not come. Friends are dying, moving, or becoming needier and less able to join in activities you once shared. Maintaining a balance in one's life and prioritizing is every bit as important as when one was younger and I believe just as challenging."

Elaine's husband Win has also has had a good fourth quarter despite a number of health and other setbacks along the way. Teamwork between them and the "will of their souls" has kept them moving in a positive direction, rather than the negative path that Jim and Carolyn encountered. They had a solid financial plan (their *How Much?*), knew their values and fourth quarter vision (their *Why?*), grew and maintained a great group of friends (their *Who?*), figured out their *Where?* as they went along and did well executing plans and pivoting (their *How?*). We all occasionally have self-inflicted wounds like Jim; how we respond to them often determines how our own story evolves and ends.

The next chapter is an overview of the key areas in which better advanced planning and good decision-making along the way can help keep difficult aging issues from turning into catastrophic fumbles.

Note when I use the terms *spouse* and *life partner*, what I'm referring to can include a common-law partner. For singles, can a close friend substitute in key areas for a spouse or life partner? The answer is yes, but not always. This is another case where "one size fits one" in the fourth quarter.

Eight Key Questions to Consider

1. How do you plan to transition well into retirement? Your spouse?

2. What is your vision of an ideal retirement? Have you discussed this vision with your friends or your life partner?

3. Do you have a clearly defined financial road map for retirement? Has it been developed with both spouses in mind? For both couples and singles, have you carefully thought through where you may be spending money?

4. How would you rate your financial advisor?

5. Is your financial advisor well versed in senior issues?

6. How well have you communicated your fourth quarter vision of life to your children?

7. How will you keep your marriage intact if you end up living longer and healthier than you expect? For singles, how will you keep your circle of friends strong and healthy as you all age?

8. Are you (and if appropriate, your spouse) on the same page when it comes to your next one or two housing choices, whether to downsize, move to an independent-care villa/ apartment, or age in place? For singles, does being single change the way you think about your long-term *Where* options?

CHAPTER 2

Keys to Fourth Quarter Happiness

Before retirement, I defined myself by my work. Now, I define myself by what I do with my free time – I'm now a grandmother, a traveler, a student learning about different cultures, a cook, and a community volunteer. I constantly look for new ways to define myself, to become who I want to be.

    – SFG fourth quarter gold-medalist client

In the following chapters, I will discuss the key areas shown by research and experience to deliver over 95% of potential happiness in the fourth quarter of our lives. Each person will do better in some areas as a result of his or her DNA, natural attitude, and disposition. Here again, one size does not fit all in fourth quarter planning. Some people will need to spend as much time learning how to improve these areas as they did studying for their educational degree decades before, keeping up with trends in their careers, or figuring out how to be better parents. Lifelong learning is critical in all stages of life, and you shouldn't stop doing it just because you're in the fourth quarter.

First, what is happiness? Happiness experts that SFG has interviewed and regularly talked with have similar messages. Happiness is a state of mind, and all of us can do things to support a better state of mind no matter our DNA or what bad cards have been dealt us or our network of friends and family by fate.

Many studies have shown that older people, usually peaking around age 65-70, are the happiest in our society. The least happy are teenagers and people in their 20s. One Stanford researcher believes that part of the reason for this is the "older and wiser" effect where older people know who they can have lunch with that will lift their spirits. The average 20 year old is less intuitive about who to have lunch with that will provide them with genuine, lasting core happiness.

The intense pursuit of happiness can backfire – for some, spending money and fulfilling bucket lists creates some short term happiness, but if they aren't improving themselves or getting more of a feeling of control in their life, or helping make someone else's life better, the happiness feeling of spending may be fleeting. Numerous studies cited in the resources section of the appendix have shown that spending a dollar on the well-being of someone else, even strangers, can increase happiness of a longer lasting variety more than spending the same dollar on yourself. Again balance is in order – spending yourself into poverty helping others worked for Mother Teresa, but doesn't work so well for most Americans. One size fits one.

Research also suggests that low expectations helps with happiness – Denmark was recently ranked as one of the happiest countries in the world, and studies show their citizens have lower overall expectations of the future. Americans have been generally raised to have higher expectations, which may account for why so many Americans focus more on what's going wrong rather than what's going right. For example, one of my high level friends in law enforcement cites how significantly safer U.S. citizens are today than just 20 years ago, despite the perception that a mass shooting could erupt in our own backyard at any given time.

This is one of many fourth quarter paradoxes – it's not in my own DNA or upbringing to suggest you lower your expectations in the fourth quarter of life just so you can be happier. In fact, you'll find many instances in this book where I encourage higher expectations. This strategy to expect a better fourth quarter has to be coupled with an "attitude of gratitude" for what you already have, or you'll find your own happiness gyrating more day-to-day than Elvis Presley's hips.

One more threat to modern happiness – the Smartphone! Turns out those valuable devices are accessed an average of 80 – 150 times per day by the average user. The negative effects on our sense of well-being, including heightened anxiety, are now being recognized.

Each of the following issues raised in this chapter will be the subject of a subsequent chapter.

Making Better Decisions

I am not a product of my circumstances. I am a product of my decisions.

– Stephen Covey

A good, solid foundation for a relationship or a home or just about anything in life makes it less likely the structure on top of the foundation will tumble when the gales of November start blowing. In this chapter I discuss the many ways our brains can trick us into making bad decisions, which often results in fumbles. *How* you figure things out was important in the first three quarters of life – your *How* becomes critical in the fourth quarter.

I will repeat many of these brain-game themes throughout the book. Most of the fumbles are caused by bad decisions that directly or indirectly lead to a fumble. Many fumbles occur as a result of making poor decisions *after* an adverse life event has disoriented us. Or thrown us to the ground.

An unavoidable fourth quarter challenge or calamity such as an early stroke or major health event may be considered a fumble by you or onlookers. It certainly can be a game-changer in your life. This book is less about the truly unavoidable fumbles, which sometimes happen for no rhyme or reason, and more about *how* to prevent the avoidable fumbles and *how* to bounce back from the unavoidable ones.

How well sharpened are your decision making skills? Those of your life partner? Do you have a history of having a good ability to bounce back after setbacks, or could your resiliency skills use some strengthening?

Having a Good Transition Plan

Progress is impossible without change, and those who cannot change their minds cannot change anything.

– George Bernard Shaw

Change is difficult. Most people need to transition to a radically new life in small steps and adjust more gradually to the changes over time. Surprisingly, less than 3% of Americans have any kind of retirement plan at all, and even fewer have a good plan for the transition from the third quarter of their lives to the fourth. Or from stage 1 (go-go) of the fourth quarter to stage 2 (slow-go), or from stage 2 to stage 3 (no-go). What makes it doubly hard is when two life partners are at different ages, stages, or on different transition patterns, which makes it more likely the relationship will destabilize, temporarily or permanently.

Having a transition plan is key to avoiding fumbles. Just figuring out when to retire can mean the difference between success and failure. Most people interpret this sentence as referring to "having enough money to retire." That is an important consideration to be sure, but being ready to retire is much more about being prepared emotionally for a whole new chapter of your life. And prepared for the dangers that lie ahead. A recent study tracked nearly half a million French people who delayed retirement. They found the people who delayed retirement had less risk of developing Alzheimer's disease or other types of dementia.

For each additional year of work, the risk of getting dementia fell by 3.2%.

"Professional activity may be an important determinant of intellectual stimulation and mental engagement, which are thought to be potentially protective against dementia," study author Dr. Carole Dufouil, a scientist at the French governmental agency INSERM, said at the Alzheimer's Association International Conference in Boston.

It's by far the largest study to look at this, and researchers say the conclusion makes sense. Working tends to keep people physically active, socially connected, and mentally challenged – all things known to help prevent mental decline.

Women naturally go through many transitions in their life. They usually, but not always, handle the first part of the fourth quarter transition stage better than men. Reasons given include good mentoring about transitions from their mothers and "It's just part of my DNA." Are women better at transitions because of nature or nurturing? One of my friends who is a leading DNA expert believes good transition planning has been programmed into women as a consequence of the transition challenges they have had to deal with over thousands of years. But he also believes the "nurture" explanation can explain some of the reason why women adjust more readily: better mentoring of daughters by their mothers than men by their fathers.

Many men we counsel were initially excited about not having day-to-day working stress and having freedom to explore their hobbies and spend more time with children and grandchildren. But shortly thereafter they get a sense of "What now?" or they get downright bored. This is the point at which many fumbles occur. Men often become too comfortable with their work defining who they are, and when they lose the work, it's as if a boat loses its rudder: steering becomes difficult, haphazard, or nonexistent. They don't look hard enough for better options in their *Why?*, their *Who?* and their *Where?* Or if they do study these areas, they sometimes don't execute them in an effective, life affirming way – your *How?* does matter!

Another key transition area to consider (usually implemented in the stage 2, or slow-go, period) is deciding if you will downsize your home, age in place (stay in your own home for as long as possible), or move into a retirement center or continuing-care retirement community, now more popularly being called *life-plan communities*.

Do you need better transition planning?

A Balanced Financial and Investment Plan

An investment in knowledge always pays the best interest.
– Benjamin Franklin

Many people in the previous generation entered the fourth quarter with pensions. They lived off Social Security and the pension, not counting on withdrawals from investment portfolios as much. For the most part, those days are gone and the financial issues when you must "make your own paycheck" are more complex than ever.

Key financial planning and investment issues include the following:

Investing allocations that take into account not only personal factors – your age, your stage of life, your financial circumstances (including how much you spend relative to your portfolio size) – but also external factors such as economic, geopolitical, and political risks that could derail your best laid plans. These external factors could also include shifts in risk versus potential return in bonds, stocks, real estate, and other asset classes; tax risks; and Super Trend forces (for instance, globalization, technology accelerators such as automation, demographics, and urbanization).

In the proverbial "old days," we were mildly concerned with Super Trends, focusing mostly on traditional best practices in planning and investing. Today, Super Trend forces affect political elections, geopolitical risk factors, economic recoveries, and portfolio risk/return relationships. They are far more critical today and their increasing speed and power affect financial-planning decisions.

How you are personally affected by inflation. The U.S. government's Consumer Price Index is based on a hypothetical spending pattern that we rarely see in real life. In recent years, things we *need* (basics of life including food and health care) have been experiencing higher inflation rates than the things we *want*, such as the latest electronic gadgets or vacation cruises. Consumer-friendly websites such as Amazon.com have made it easier for shoppers to compare prices, putting unprecedented power in the hands of consumers. Good for fourth quarter consumers and one of the reasons that inflation pressures have been lower in recent years.

If your go-go and slow-go years are extended, do you have enough set aside and invested properly to buy the same loaf of bread and jug of milk (or health care) 20 years from now when they may cost 50% more (or possibly higher) than they cost today?

How do you balance living well in your go-go years versus your slow-go years? Some people after 9/11 decided life is short and uncertain, so they would live it up more in the go-go years. There is something to be said for this approach, living well while your health permits. But moderation is also important, especially so if you have more limited financial resources.

Are your assets and finances set up to provide the margin of safety you need as you reach various milestones in the fourth quarter? Do you have a good, well researched plan for How Much you need?

Having a Good Reason to Get Out of Bed

If you think adventure is dangerous, try routine. It is lethal.
– Paulo Coehlo

Note that the above chapter heading includes the word *good*. This is your all-important *Why?* When people didn't live as long in the fourth quarter of their lives, having a reason to get out of bed wasn't as critical. By the time they had played enough golf and tennis and travelled, they were getting chronic ailments that limited their mobility and lifestyle. If you have 20 good years ahead of you at age 65, with minimal chronic ailments, what would you do to stay engaged in life and feel your life has a higher purpose?

Have you filled out your "bucket list" of things that you want to do before you die or get too old to enjoy them? It turns out this is the source of many fumbles in the fourth quarter! An interesting article in the *Wall Street Journal* profiled research showing that many people become so obsessed with their bucket to-do list that they spend less time with children and grandchildren (and sometimes even their life partners), creating the very disaster they thought they were avoiding.

The Bank of America/ML 2016 *Leisure in Retirement: Beyond the Bucket List* study found that retirees value fun and quality time with friends and family above all, and in 2015 they spent more on travel and leisure than any other age group. The study found that:

- 88% viewed retirement as a new beginning instead of an ending.
- 66% prefer to try new things rather than sticking to old hobbies or pastimes.
- 95% prefer to purchase experiences rather than things.

As the fourth quarter progresses into the stage 3 no-go years nearer the end of life, most people begin to reflect on what they will leave as a legacy in the world. For many it's their children and grandchildren, hopefully happy, healthy, and employed. For others it's helping their favorite community cause and perhaps even setting up a donor-advised fund at a community foundation. For those with a higher net worth, setting up their own private foundations may be part of their legacy planning.

Do you have a compelling reason to stay engaged with the world as you age?

Wellness versus the Absence of Illness

80% of healthy respondents were "very satisfied" after 15 years of retirement, compared to 25% who were in poor health.

— 2016 EBRI research study

The good news is that the current generation of Americans entering the fourth quarter is the healthiest generation ever despite the obesity epidemic mentioned earlier. One cancer expert recently described to me many forms of cancer as "chronic, treatable ailments," with good reason to believe that more diseases will be treatable, even curable, in the near future. Even a history of poor family health may become, well, history in the next decade. Scientists are learning how to repair genes that spelled trouble for previous generations.

Alzheimer's disease, one of the most feared maladies in the fourth quarter right beside cancer, may also become a chronic treatable disease in the near future. An incredible amount of research is being done and some traction towards slowing down the disease has been achieved. Stopping it altogether and reversing Alzheimer's and dementia is a more daunting challenge also being worked on by researchers around the planet.

Here is one of many promising recent breakthroughs. A team of German researchers has developed a blood test that could detect Alzheimer's at a very early stage. This breakthrough was highlighted in the *Journal of Biophotonics* and further details were published in the journal, *Analytical Chemistry*. Why is this important? Drugs are in various stages of development that can significantly inhibit the progress of Alzheimer's disease. Many of these drugs need to be taken in the early stages of dementia forming. This blood test detects changes up to fifteen years before clinical symptoms. It achieved a diagnostic precision of 84 percent in the blood and 90 percent in spinal fluid. Currently, sample analyses for early detection in another 800 study participants are being conducted.

There is no question that medical science is progressing more rapidly than ever and that early detection of disease is both important and being accomplished, but only if you're getting checked regularly. The Internet of Things (IoT for short) promises to bring us regular monitoring of vital functions. The Qualcomm "tricorder" challenge helped create a whole new generation of diagnostic tools that are being refined for next generation disease detection.

The bad news is that technological advances are also creating a more sedentary society, good nutrition habits have been overwhelmed by foods that addict our minds and taste buds, the health-care system has become difficult to navigate, many people are on multiple pharmaceuticals with many side effects, and even one serious health problem can derail even the best exercise and nutrition plan. This can create a cascade effect: The positive elements of life can be destabilized by aging problems, creating even more challenges. Many seniors find themselves less resilient to change and adversity, although this risk can be reduced with the right actions.

One of the best proactive steps you can take is to create a baseline of key health areas needed to stay well and identify problems in your body or mind early. An annual physical with your local physician can provide early detection of treatable diseases.

Those who want to get serious about their health screens in the fourth quarter will likely want to do a full workup with their primary-care practitioner or at a major health facility like Duke (Durham, North Carolina), the Cleveland Clinic (Cleveland, Ohio), the Mayo Clinic (Rochester, Minnesota; Jacksonville, Florida; and Phoenix, Arizona), or the pioneer of early disease prevention and wellness, the Cooper Clinic in Dallas, Texas. These programs are surprisingly affordable, especially when compared to the high cost of health problems in dollars and in lost life opportunities.

Many people believe their goal is to get patched up quickly when they have a health problem. The medical establishment is good at this even though many misdiagnoses still continue despite progress in better diagnostic technologies. The best approach is to pursue wellness instead of just fixing illnesses as they occur. A good side effect of wellness is it can decrease your health costs in the fourth quarter and make you want to stay engaged with your Why? and your Who?, your spouse, family, and your friends, over a longer period of time. Positive cascade effects like this create much better fourth quarter outcomes.

Some walking, strength training, and general exercise will help you fend off illness but not necessarily create wellness. The *Younger Next Year* authors cite many studies that indicate an aggressive health-care fitness program can reduce the chance of a major illness by 70%. We all have known people who were fitness nuts and still died early, so this is no guarantee. But tilting the odds in your favor every chance you get decreases your odds of a major fumble as you age.

The best wellness prescription is to create a doable, aggressive fitness program that includes regular exercise such as walking and strength training and at least four aerobic workouts every week that cause your heart rate go to 70% of maximum for at least 45 minutes.

Are you pursing wellness or just settling for not being ill? Is your exercise program challenging enough? Do you have a competent health-care advocate to help you navigate the health-care system?

Social Networks Rule Even in the Fourth Quarter

If you're always trying to be normal, you'll never know how amazing you can be.
– Maya Angelou

Good professional and social networks have long been associated with success in life and careers. It turns out that fourth quarter success still requires good networks to be at the top of your game! This is the *Who?* – the people that you spend time with matter to your fourth quarter success.

In the digital age, location still matters when it comes to maintaining good networks of friends and resources. Over time, even the best network changes because of chronic illness, death, and divorce. A number of people I interviewed in the mid-stage of the fourth quarter talked about how many friends they have "lost" as a result of them moving away to be closer to their own family. Our friendship garden needs to be tended regularly, especially because many people don't make as many new, close friends as they progress into and through the fourth quarter.

If you haven't paid attention to your mental and physical wellness program and have become the quintessential grumpy old man or anxious old woman, it won't be surprising if your network of friends shrinks and shrivels over time: yet another example where inattention to one area causes fumbles in another.

If you have divorced or lost your mate, remarrying in this stage should be done with eyes wide open and some background research done on your intended companion or spouse. Wealthier individuals should consider hiring professionals to do background checks. Romantic it's not, but it can save you from one of the most disastrous fourth quarter fumbles, elder abuse. Many cases of elder abuse happen as a result of a remarriage in later life.

How would you rate your social support network?

Communicate Until the Cows Come Home

The most important thing in communication is hearing what isn't said.
– Peter Drucker

Communication with spouses and with family members has many new ways to become strained during the fourth quarter. Simply dealing with tough transition issues and feelings of losing your identity can create significant emotions that take over in conversations with your life partner, friends, and family members.

What factors are at play when people of high IQ fail in the fourth quarter and those of modest IQ succeed? Apparently, an outstanding IQ is not a good predictor of fourth quarter success and a strong EQ (emotional intelligence) is a better predictor. **EQ is critical for making intelligent *How?* decisions.** Key EQ factors include self-awareness, self-regulation, motivation, empathy, and social skills. If one or more of these is not at a good or higher level, it's pretty certain you'll encounter more fumbles that you would like in the fourth quarter.

In the communication chapter, I'll give you some ideas for better communication and EQ skills in the fourth quarter even if that's never been your strong suit.

Are your communication skills up to the challenges of the fourth quarter?

Thoughtful Estate Planning

It is always wise to look ahead, but difficult to look further than you can see.

– Winston Churchill

Most people think of estate planning as having a will or avoiding as much tax as possible when passing assets to the next generation. Over two-thirds of Americans don't have a will (this number jumps to almost three-quarters for minorities), and many need to think more about what happens as the fourth quarter progresses, not just when the buzzer sounds at the end of life. What if you become incapacitated? Can your spouse handle all the health-care and financial decisions? Is there any danger of elder abuse, with one of your family members bleeding your estate dry?

Recent changes in tax law have made fewer estates subject to estate tax, although there are many other hidden taxes that need to be considered and reduced if possible.

Have you updated your estate plan lately? Considered where it might fail?

Getting Your Living Options Right

It's a funny thing coming home. Nothing changes. Everything feels the same, even smells the same. You realize what's changed is you.

– F. Scott Fitzgerald

I've devoted an entire chapter to long-term living options because so many fourth quarter fumbles happen in this area. Good planning for long-term care involves much more to think about than just whether you have long-term-care insurance. Paying for lifestyle options is important, but over 90% of the fumbles we see in senior-living choices are made by people who can readily afford good care.

Most of the people I work with want to age in place in their home as long as possible. This is likely a more costly choice, and in some cases, especially where dementia is involved, it can be downright dangerous. But for some, this is the best option in terms of comfortable surroundings and the desire to be "in the mainstream population" as long as possible.

Do you have a general idea of your future living alternatives in the fourth quarter living? Have you considered or explored options?

Consider a Different Future

In the first chapter, Jim and Carolyn's story was one of fumbles leading to more fumbles. Let's look at Joe and Barbara's story, which has the potential for fumbles, but how a little advanced planning, combined with a more intentional *How Much?, Why?, Who? and Where?,* connected by smart *How?* decisions, led to a much happier and fun fourth quarter, closer to their dreams.

> **The first potential fumble (and perhaps more), avoided:** Joe was a well-respected executive – he had a team that looked up to him, trusted him, and went the extra mile. Joe started considering his "next chapter" options when he was two years out from retirement. He had breakfasts and lunches with friends who were retired, and asked them if they knew other people he should talk with. He found that about half of his growing network kept working at some level for pay, and they seemed to be the happier group.

Joe and Barbara's financial plan showed they could live off their assets and social security, but would do better and have a larger margin of safety if they could extend Joe's income into the fourth quarter. For Joe, this made the decision easy – happier + better margin of safety = better fourth quarter. Joe decided to take a consulting job that used his previous skills in a different way.

Here is how Joe completed his time chart [blank version in the Appendix] to replace his five "work days":

- **Two days a week using his skills to make money for the next 5-10 years, health permitting,**
- **One day a week, spread out over the week, focused on his health,**
- **One day a week focused on doing special things with Barbara, the children and grandchildren, in addition to devoting weekends to family,**
- **One day a week indulging himself with golf, catching up with friends, reading and keeping himself sharp.**

The plan worked well during the first 6 months, but then the winds of fate had other plans. His consulting business was taking off and he had hired several extra virtual consultants to help cover the load. Exercising took a back seat and his regular check-ins every two weeks with friends degraded into hit or miss connections.

Joe was carried away with his *Why?* and didn't realize that too much of a good thing can result in fumbles. Barbara thought this was the life Joe wanted, so she didn't say much as Joe's week drifted back towards his old schedule where she only got his full attention on weekends.

Joe found himself back in the midst of exciting projects, but not feeling fulfilled. His weight was going up and his attitude was occasionally surly. His ego was being stroked every day but his balance wheel was out of alignment. His *Why?* wasn't where he wanted it to be. After a long conversation with me and some of his best friends, including Barbara, he decided to carve off part of his consulting business and give it to one of his consultants. Joe used his *Who?* network well, and even added a few good friends that proved vital for future stages of his life in the fourth quarter. He thought about and executed his *How?* decisions well.

Revisiting his core purpose and values, he decided to add community work into the mix:

- **One day a week using his skills to make money for the next 3-5 years, health permitting,**
- **One day a week helping community causes that he enjoyed working with during his regular working years,**
- **One day a week, spread out over the week, focused on his health,**
- **One day a week focused on doing special things with Barbara, the children and grandchildren, in addition to devoting weekends to family,**
- **One day a week indulging himself with golf, catching up with friends, reading and keeping himself sharp.**

Looking back on this early part of his fourth quarter, Joe believes he avoided several major fumbles. They included replacing one stressful job for another, having Barbara and his family not respect him or his decision making as much, declining health and losing touch with dear friends. He also discovered that one particular community group needed some specialized skills to grow its mission – he engaged with them and helped they triple their impact in the community over the next five years. A major *How?* and *Why?* win that wouldn't have happened if he had just written checks to his favorite cause.

The second potential fumble (and perhaps more), avoided: Barbara was not feeling fully satisfied with her life. Joe's struggles to get his balance right in the first part of his fourth quarter destabilized her as she tried to adjust to his changing schedule.

She found herself getting angry at times and depressed other times. Her schedule looked like this:

- **A half day a week, spread out over the week, focused on her health.**
- **Three days a week focused on doing special things with the children and grandchildren, and sometimes Joe, in addition to devoting weekends to family.**
- **A half day a week indulging herself with Mahjongg and bridge, catching up with friends, reading and keeping herself sharp.**
- **One day a week for household chores, occasionally changed due to Joe's schedule.**

When we had worked on Barbara's values and future options, her own "true north" *Why?* was less defined by Joe – she had really wanted to get more engaged with a particular community group, help out one of the children by watching the grandchildren occasionally and travelling more.

While Joe was having his adjustment issues early in the fourth quarter, she decided she needed to be more intentional with her own dreams. She had been doing some volunteering with a community group that meant a lot to her. She sat down with the director of the group and brainstormed on things she could do that would match her passions and time constraints. She talked about the options with me, with Joe and with friends. She used her good *Who?* network to full effect, and figured out *how* to make her dream a reality.

She scheduled trips every couple of months to be with her children that allowed her to do fun things with the grandchildren, while also giving the children a break for date nights and travelling.

Barbara found several interesting trips on the internet and invited several girl friends to go along. She had a great week away to a place where she had always wanted to go.

Reflecting on this period of time, Barbara is sure she would have had several fumbles if she hadn't taken action and kept herself grounded as Joe struggled with his own life balance. She believes that her mental and physical health would have suffered, and she would have developed more resentment that Joe hadn't done a better job thinking out his own early transition plan, making her own life more unpredictable and less fun. Fast forward and the community group she devoted more time to has grown in no small part because of her time, passion and energy and is a large part of her "slow-go" years. She is proud not only of her fourth quarter accomplishments, but the fact that she figured out *how* to make it happen through her networking and her own ingenuity.

When Joe got his life stabilized, he and Barbara had several good "next chapter" planning sessions with me. They moved to a weekly schedule that was good for Joe, good for Barbara and good for them as a couple.

> **The third potential fumble (and perhaps more), avoided:**
> A financial crisis arrived. Joe and Barbara were both well versed in what financial metrics were key to their future success, so they were focused on how the crisis would affect these metrics. Turns out they had a good balance in their portfolio and in their spending and didn't feel compelled to make major moves right away. Only a few small adjustments to "the set of their sails" and they achieved a good "eat well, sleep well" balance. They were able to navigate through the financial storm without major cuts to their fun plan for the future.
>
> Looking back, they see so many friends who experienced multiple fumbles that destabilized health plans along with financial plans. No telling how many fumbles they might have experienced if they hadn't been more proactive about their *How Much?* finances.

The fourth potential fumble (and perhaps more), avoided:
Barbara and Joe's original *Where?* plan had been to downsize
their home when they were deeper into retirement, perhaps 10
to 15 years out. Joe hoped they could stay in their home as long
as possible. As their mobility declined, they became more intentional looking at downsizing options. After two years of talking
with realtors and identifying their ideal location and home type,
they found the solution that both are happy with.

They paid $1,000 and are on the waiting list for a Life Care com-
munity. It may take 5 years or longer before their ideal villa or
apartment becomes available. In the meantime, they continue
to focus on their modified (now mostly combined) "slow-go"
weekly schedule:

- **One day a week, spread out over the
  week, focused on their health,**
- **One day a week focused on doing special things
  with the children and grandchildren. Weekends are
  often split between family and fun activities,**
- **One day a week involved in their own
  respective community activities,**
- **One day a week indulging themselves in hobbies, catching
  up with friends, reading and keeping themselves sharp,**
- **One day a week for household chores, with duties
  split between both of them. The downsized home has
  made all of these activities often take only half a day
  a week, allowing more time for other fun activities.**

Joe and Barbara are maintaining pretty good life balance wheels
in their "slow-go" years despite repeated health events that have
become more serious as they progress deeper into the fourth
quarter. Both have been told by their physicians that early diagnosis, along with both being in good physical shape, have been

the key to why they have survived and bounced back better than others when recovering from surgical procedures.

The fifth potential fumble, so far avoided: Both are seeing friends in their *Who?* network move away, become infirmed or housebound, or get sick and die. As a result of their more proactive *Who?* efforts to replant their friends garden, they've both still have quite a few friends that they see for lunch or enjoy doing a variety of activities together.

Now late in the "slow-go" years, there remain a number of potential fumble issues. One of their children went through a tough divorce and needs more help, financially and emotionally. A grandchild has health problems and they are spending more time with them, as well as using their elder wisdom and financial resources to help look for more solutions to cure him. No doubt other unknowns lie ahead in their journey, but they feel in control of their own ship's destiny and still have good resources in the *How Much?*, *Why?*, *Who?* and *Where?* focus areas. And they have confidence in their ability to figure out *how* to make the tough decisions that may lie ahead.

CHAPTER 3

Making Better Decisions

If I had an hour to solve a problem and my life depended on the solution, I would spend the first 55 minutes determining the proper question to ask, for once I know the proper question, I could solve the problem in less than five minutes.

– Albert Einstein

Asking the right questions in the fourth quarter can be critical to finding the right solutions unique to you. If you have a life partner, this chapter applies to them too; your partner is a vital part of why you may have more success than failure in the fourth quarter. The *"How Much?"* and the *"Why?"* and the *"Who?"* – and at some point the *"Where?"* – all connected by a well-considered *How?* approach, are all vital to answer and, at times, reimagine and answer in a different way.

Making the right decisions at key junctures, as well as seemingly small decisions made every week, is critical to fourth quarter success. Once you have a better idea of your fourth quarter values, making better decisions will be easier but not always easy. As your brain functions slow down, fumbles resulting from poor decision-making become more prevalent.

There is a growing industry intent on helping people keep their brains sharper and creative in the fourth quarter. This includes the current leader of this field, Lumosity.com, which purports to have 70 million "brain trainers" in 182 countries challenging their brains to improve. The Lumosity "fit test" scores you in speed of solving puzzles and in ability in train-of-thought and memory skills as compared to others your own age. These exercises are in the "do no harm" category and are perhaps even helpful in warding off brain decline.

Studies of the Mankato nuns by the Sanders Brown Center on Aging at the University of Kentucky even suggest intense brain exercise, learning a new language, and earning a college degree later in life can rewire parts of the brain and diminish the effects of certain kinds of dementia.

The *Younger Next Year* authors cite good research that shows that better blood circulation through better fitness will make it easier to stay sharp mentally. This notion is supported by many of the leading aging and medical gerontology experts that I interviewed.

But there is another series of "This is your brain. This is your brain in the fourth quarter" issues that are critical in determining success or failure later in life.

Asking the right questions may not lead to the best outcomes if our decision process is flawed. You can "know" that your *Why?* and *Who?* decisions are important, but if you don't get the *How?* decision making process done well, you'll still experience fumbles. Turns out, most people have flawed decision-making skills. The brain is an amazing tool but, like a chainsaw, it can reach unfortunate outcomes if the operator's attention wanders or if it is left to run in a random direction. *Even more disconcerting is the fact that the normal brain-pattern approaches that served us well earlier in life can get us into trouble in the fourth quarter.*

Research attempting to understand why patterned thinking can lead us down the wrong path came up with four primary reasons:

- The desire for control
- The desire to be viewed by ourselves and the world as rational
- The effort to suppress negative feelings and regrets
- The effort to maximize winning and minimize losing

Unfortunately, we have seen multiple fourth quarter fumbles that originated from one or more of these four areas, many of which were programmed into the subconscious in the first 5 to 10 years of life. My team at Stearns Financial runs workshops on "Money scripts": views on money that were programmed in our subconscious minds when we were young by parents, aunts, uncles, or friends. Money scripts can be dangerous autopilot software inside us that create money mistakes, but there are also non-money scripts of all kinds running in our minds that can sabotage our best efforts to make good decisions.

In the wonderful book *Thinking Fast and Slow*, Nobel Economics prize winner Daniel Kahneman took these four desire and effort areas to a whole new level. There are numerous examples in the book of how the "fast brain," the one that handles everyday tasks quickly and efficiently, is used too often to answer questions when the "slow brain" should have been engaged. Even if you try to follow the advice in each of the fumble-avoidance techniques discussed in this book, you might find yourself making fundamental-decision mistakes too often and you may find yourself saying, "I knew better than that" or "I should have considered a different approach." *That's your cue to explore why you made the decision you did so you can make better decisions going forward.*

Kaizen: Powerful Tool in Life and the Fourth Quarter

After studying dozens of research studies on failure in the fourth quarter, and witnessing dozens of clients, friends, and others stumble and fall later in life, it's clear that adapting to change becomes tougher as we age. You're probably thinking something along the lines of, "Duh, who didn't already know that?" But knowing and doing something about adapting better to change are two entirely different things.

Some of us may be older and wiser from our life experiences, but the speed of change in the world heightens anxiety for many later in life. On top of this change-anxiety, if your life habits over many decades make fumbles more likely, how can you adapt better at the very time that it may make the difference between having a happy, fulfilling fourth quarter and one filled with misery and fear?

One different approach embedded in each of the 25 fumbles in this book, and the additional 25 profiled at the www.FourthQuarterFumbles. com website, is the Japanese concept of Kaizen, taking small baby steps towards your goals and toward change. Americans marvel at the big, bold innovation moves of a Bill Gates, Jeff Bezos, or Steve Jobs. *But try big and bold in diets, exercise, or just about any endeavor where we're trying to effect sustainable change and failure is more the norm than success.*

Part of the reason for this change-failure is the primal areas of our brain that trigger a fear response. Ten thousand years ago, fear of being eaten by wild animals drove our actions to run like the wind. Today, the 24/7 media machine of cable, radio and internet stokes the fires of fear every day all day unlike anything we've seen in history. Where do we run? We fear terrorism as if it were lurking outside our homes when in fact greater dangers, such as heart disease, and texting while driving, kill far more people every year than terrorist acts.

If we try to make too large a change in the fourth quarter, the same fear-center of our brain sabotages our efforts to effect positive change. Fear of success has been researched for many years and is well understood today. As we move from one stage of our life to another, physically or emotionally, we often realize that we are outside of our comfort zone. This creates fear at many subconscious levels.

Fears include letting ourselves or other people we care about down, humiliation, and even losing the fourth quarter game and being judged by future generations of our family. Fear triggers flight chemistry in our brain and sabotages the very thing we want and need to change. Success is a risk.

Kaizen, making small steps towards change, doesn't raise fear to the level where our primal brains say "Run!" Instead, the primal brain stays inactive watching for other dangers that may be lurking. There are small-step solutions to every fumble in this book. The key is to determine if they are *your* best small-step solutions.

Kaizen can be a secret *How?* puzzle key.

In his terrific book *Nine Things You Simply Must Do to Succeed in Love and in Life*, Henry Cloud calls Kaizen "acting like an ant": the practice of taking small steps to accomplish large tasks. The principle decreases the risk of feeling overwhelmed while encouraging the individual by shifting the focus to small accomplishments. Dr. Cloud sums it up as one of life's great paradoxes: *wanting things quickly can cause you to miss getting them at all.*

Cloud-based Solutions

No, we're not going to launch into a discussion of how the technology cloud is changing our lives in what Microsoft's software genius Craig Mundie calls, "the greatest change supernova of our lifetime." Instead, let's take a look at how Dr. Cloud's nine principles can help us avoid brain fumbles. His work is based on studying successful people's lives and can be instrumental in helping us avoid fumbles in the fourth quarter. These successful people all:

- Had healthy relationships
- Reached their goals
- Did not repeat the same mistakes
- Were in control of their lives
- Felt a sense of purpose

Sound like a good recipe for preparing your brain for fourth quarter success?

The first principle, "***Dig it Up***," is the practice of self-awareness. In the fourth quarter, we must honestly examine any weaknesses we have, process them, and then determine how we can overcome them to avoid fumbles. *Then look at our strengths, take an honest inventory of our passions and talents, develop them, face any fears, and take calculated risks to find our Why?* Do this well and you will get *fourth quarter bonus points* – you will find a lot more interesting *Who?* people to hang around.

The second principle, "***Pull the Tooth***," is the practice of confronting problems and letting them go. The key concept is that avoidance is unhealthy and limiting. I have found that people who have a successful fourth quarter of life do not allow unhealthy negative situations to linger; *they face the issues, make tough decisions, avoid negative people (an important Who? concept!), and then move on with their lives.*

The third principle, "**Play the Movie**," is the practice of beginning with the end in mind before making decisions. This is a key practice I've used for decades in my scenario work in investing, financial planning, and business practices. By actively visualizing a potential positive or negative outcome, we increase our capacity for effective decision-making. *Dr. Cloud suggests seeing, planning, and then evaluating each scene "in light of where we want the movie to end."* Then move in that direction and consider every decision you make in the context of your preferred future.

The fourth principle, "**Do Something**," is the practice of taking personal responsibility. Successful people in the fourth quarter call on themselves to *correct difficult situations regardless of whether they are to blame for creating the situation.* Although painful circumstances and difficult people are often out of our control, the ability to respond healthily to these challenges is always within one's control. Cloud highlights the importance of the principle by explaining that freedom results from "ownership and responsibility."

The fifth principle, "**Act like an Ant**," is the very important but underappreciated Kaizen practice, previously highlighted, of *taking small steps to accomplish large tasks without triggering the primal parts of your brain intent on limiting your ability to embrace change.*

The sixth principle, "**Hate Well**," sounds surprising in a world of greater conflict. This principle is the practice of hating in a way that solves problems instead of creating them. *"Character is in part formed by what we hate, because we move to be different from* *whatever that is."* Cloud suggests that hating well preserves life and that hating poorly destroys life.

An integral component of hating well is objectivity, which hates the issue without hating the person. There are many things that we hate about growing old – especially the life-and-death issues that we must confront. *Avoiding fumbles in the fourth quarter is easier if you don't take your anger out on those you love.* Hating poorly is also a good way to drive away the most important people in your *Who?* network.

The seventh principle, "**Don't Play Fair**," is another curious title since we are all taught by our parents to play fair with our siblings and friends. In this context it means the practice of loving unconditionally. *Loving without conditions is unfair in an eye-for-an-eye world and incredibly powerful.*

Cloud suggests that loving without conditions is possible only when healthy detachment exists. Fourth quarter fumbles often occur as we become too critical of the shortcomings of others – or because our fears cause us to become too clingy to those we love. Its normal and natural to accelerate good and bad feelings with our life partner when we are spending way more time with them than at any point in the past; too much of a good thing is usually not a good thing. Cloud's advice: *"Give back better than you're given."*

The eighth principle, "**Be Humble**," is the practice of serving and learning. Arrogance denies failure, avoids correction, and fears criticism, all of which undermine learning, a key to avoiding fourth quarter fumbles. *Be more concerned with what is right instead of who is right.* This can help you maintain a healthy *Who?* network, succeed more in your *Why?* efforts, avoid a number of fourth quarter fumbles, including the rising trend of divorce in the fourth quarter, also called gray divorce.

The ninth principle, "**Upset the Right People**," is the practice of risking the loss of the approval of others. Doesn't this conflict with the idea of building your social network stronger and better in the fourth quarter? Not at all. Disconnecting from the emotional response of others is critical to healthy decisions and healthy relationships. Let's say one of your good friends of over 30 years begins to exhibit all the toxic behaviors that create fourth quarter fumbles. You want to help them but you find that their toxicity is affecting your own mind-set. Stand by your principles even if it means risking the relationship with a friend. *Part of developing new Who? networks in the fourth quarter includes periodically weeding the garden.*

Do you recognize the emotional intelligence, or EQ, factors previously discussed in these principles? None of these nine principles are particularly easy to follow at times in our lives. *How* you follow these principles is more important than memorizing them. If we haven't done well in these areas in the first three quarters, how can we succeed at making them better in the fourth quarter? *Figure it out and you will experience uncommon success in the last chapter of your life. If not now, when?*

Making Better Fourth Quarter Decisions

Here are some ideas for making better decisions in the fourth quarter:

Make a puzzle out of a problem. When we recognize that we have a problem, we want to fix it right away. We want to quickly find a solution. The next time you encounter a real or potential fourth quarter problem, turn it into a puzzle. Our brains were taught at an early stage to engage at a different level (the *slow brain*, using Kahneman's terminology) on a puzzle. First, we reframe the issues and consider different ways the puzzle could play out – or how the movie will play out using scenario learning. This simple technique can prevent many fourth quarter dangers, including leaping quickly to a solution, being in a fixed and rigid mind-set, and eliminating potentially good ideas before they have been fully examined.

Admit being right isn't the goal. Many people live the first three quarters of their lives in multiple contests. Whether in school or at work, we assumed our job was to be more right than the person next to us in order to excel. Many fourth quarter fumbles that I've witnessed were from people who leaped to a solution, found it wasn't working right, but didn't change the approach because of pride or ego.

Look at the situation from an objective observer's viewpoint. Better yet, listen more closely to friends and family members when they have critiques of you. You may not like the picture but consider the critiques as if your five lifelong heroes (for instance, one of your parents, your most grounded best friend, Abraham Lincoln, Ben Franklin, and Eleanor Roosevelt) were looking at the puzzle and providing their feedback.

When you allow yourself to find a different perspective that seems to work, give yourself permission to consider the new perspective. This approach is considered one of the best to avoid brain-induced fourth quarter mistakes.

Just do it! The opposite of using the fast-thinking brain to solve complex problems is when the slow-thinking brain engages and never allows you to make a decision, good or bad. Its "Ready, aim, aim, aim . . ." and never "fire." We've found many engineers trained to think deeper fall into this trap in the fourth quarter. Taking small steps towards the goal after doing your homework and communicating well with others involved in the decision can help overcome analysis paralysis.

Another trap in this area is the feeling of needing to be safe (the reason staying in one's home deep into the fourth quarter is seductive) or the fear of making a mistake. These are normal, primal feelings that can become magnified in the fourth quarter if we're not careful.

Don't settle for mediocre results. A subtler form of fourth quarter fumbles is when someone settles for a solution that doesn't seem quite right overall but seems to be economical, efficient, or "isn't worth fighting about." Or is it? Consider carefully decisions using the techniques above. If you have a nagging feeling you may be headed down the wrong path, reconsider your options, talk with friends, and don't be afraid to reopen the discussion with your life partner over a decision that's already been made so you can feel good that it's the best decision you can make with the information you have at hand.

Beware of common decision villains. In their book *Decisive: How to Make Better Choices in Life and Work*, Chip and Dan Heath do a wonderful job of describing the four villains of decision-making: narrow framing, confirmation bias, short-term emotion, and overconfidence. I believe that the last villain can be even more insidious in the fourth quarter when it goes from overconfidence to underconfidence.

Take baby steps. Use the Japanese concept of kaizen. What is the simplest thing (*How* matters!) you can do to move towards a better future?

Top financial planners and advisors are trained in helping their clients think through fourth quarter puzzles. They can help you frame up the right questions, provide resources to consider puzzle solutions, and act as a general sounding board for making better decisions. Often, they find perceptions such as, "I can't afford that" are really just fast-brain money scripts. When thoughtful alternative scenarios are examined, a solution may magically surface that is both affordable and better suited to happiness in the fourth quarter.

We will now dive into the top 25 fumbles to understand and ideally avoid in the fourth quarter of your life. An additional set of fumbles are discussed at the end of each chapter that can be reviewed at www.FourthQuarterFumbles.com. Even though the 25 "red zone" fumbles profiled in this book are the most prevalent, it's good to know the entire 50 fumble set since you may inadvertently be positioned for a lower likelihood fumble.

Potential Red-Zone Fumble #1: Poor Decision-Making

If there is one thing that will fundamentally change our lives in the fourth quarter for better or worse, it's the decisions we make every day. Some are big decisions, like *how* to keep ourselves engaged in the first stage of the fourth quarter without destabilizing our relationship with friends and loved ones. Some are smaller decisions, like whether we skip walking today or eating right. Every decision we make moves us closer or farther away from our ideal vision of the fourth quarter.

Making better decisions involves many of the principles discussed in this chapter. Making *better informed* decisions is a critical add-on skill many of us have learned in the previous stages of our lives but sometimes don't do as well in the fourth quarter when we're thrown unfamiliar boomerangs to either catch or duck!

Avoiding fumbles: Sharpen your decision-making skills, especially in the all-important *How?* area. Read *Decisive* by the Heath brothers. This book highlights the four villains of decision-making and *how* to outsmart and overcome the villains.

Learn *how* your friends and others have made better decisions in the fourth quarter of their lives and adapt the approaches to your own unique way of doing things. Be more mindful of decisions you make.

Recovering fumbles: Made a really bad decision? You're not alone! That's a great time to figure out *how* and *what* you could have done differently and work towards getting back on a good path towards your ideal fourth quarter.

Dangers: More fumbles. Less happiness. Life partner disagreements. Gray divorce. Developing anxiety or depression.

Action plan: Be a student of good decision-making. Hang around people who make better decisions. Listen beyond the *what* to the *how* they go about making and executing decisions. Especially seek out people who have faced adversity, made good decisions, and have already experienced the decision process you're getting ready to face.

Mars/Venus considerations: Men and women have equal opportunities for fumbles in different ways because both usually have more difficulty in different areas of decision-making. Men tend to be overconfident of their decision-making skills, and women tend to be underconfident. "Stay in your lane" means focusing on areas you're best in and letting your life partner (or friends or paid helpers) focus on areas where you are not as naturally strong.

The "growth" mind-set suggests trying things that require new learning. Ideally, this doesn't involve rewiring the bathroom fan if you've never done it before.

Special issues for singles: Some people lose their confidence in their decision-making after becoming single, whether by choice (divorce) or fate (death of a spouse). It's critical you maintain confidence in the fourth quarter and surround yourself with others who can help with decision-making. Making an effort to understand your future options (being an informed consumer) and sharpening your own decision skills for the fourth quarter can help you build confidence.

Kaizen (small steps to success) ideas: Ask one person you have observed make consistently good decisions *how* he or she does it. Even one better decision made per week can build up to a large positive impact in the fourth quarter.

Potential Red-Zone Fumble #2:
Poor Resiliency Skills

Every new beginning comes from some other beginning's end.

— Seneca, Roman philosopher

American culture teaches and celebrates the person who gets knocked down, gets back up, and wins the big game. It can be harder in real life to get back up, dust off, and thrive after a major life calamity. If you're experiencing the onset of boredom or chronic illness in the fourth quarter, your bounce-back ability can be even more strained.

The Resilience Factor: 7 Keys to Finding your Inner Strength and Overcoming Life's Hurdles by Karen Reivich and Andrew Shatte has many good ideas about how to overcome adversity and become a happy, well-adjusted person: "Resilience transforms. It transforms hardship into challenge, failure into success, helplessness into power."

Based on years of research, this book connects our reactions to certain adversities with our instincts, showing that the brain is programmed to respond in particular ways, a theme of this book's entire third chapter. These evolutionary responses help us to solve problems by understanding their cause, challenge how we think about future adversities, and build our resilience to adversity.

The authors offer seven steps to build your resilience, showing that it is something that can be learned; it's not just an innate ability. "The foundation of the seven skills of resilience is built on the simple realization that our emotions and behaviors are triggered not by events themselves but by how we interpret those events."

The seven steps for building resilience are:

Learn your ABCs. When confronted with adversity, listen to your thoughts, identify what you say to yourself when faced with a challenge, and understand how your thoughts affect your feelings and behavior.

Avoid thinking traps. Don't make the thinking mistakes previously highlighted that undermine resilience.

Detect icebergs. Identify your deep, maybe hidden, beliefs and determine when they help and when they hurt you.

Challenge beliefs. This is Brain Games 101. Find new problem-solving/thinking strategies in order to avoid undermining yourself and pursuing the wrong solutions.

Put it in perspective. Stop thinking about "What if?" and perceiving every failure as a catastrophe. Even though I've been called the scenario guy and our firm has been recognized as a scenario leader, this mirrors my own belief that too many scenarios and watching too many "What if?" talking heads on TV is bad for mental health!

Stay calm and focused. It is important to stay calm and focused when overwhelmed by stress or emotion. This can be hard when a life partner or sibling or friend is always overreacting to crises.

Develop better real-time resilience. Change your counterproductive thoughts into more resilient ones. You'll find many good examples for the fourth quarter in this book.

A Buddhist friend, who has spent half the fourth quarter trying to understand resiliency, framed it this way:

Everyone's life will include unpleasant experiences. The aversion to the unpleasantness is what often makes it hard to bounce back. We want our lives to be different. When life hits us hard, we need to change our response to the bad experience. If we can acknowledge unpleasant feelings, be with them, and let them run their course, we've built a better bounce-back system.

This is easier said than done. It requires mindfulness. *When I could be consciously aware, "This shattered relationship with my son is hard to bear" and not add the sentence in my head, "Life's not fair" or countlessly replay what I could have done differently years ago to avoid the fumble, then I've moved towards acceptance and tranquility. Whenever I've longed for bad feelings to go away and be replaced with good feelings, the longing itself has impeded my healing process.*

My religion also teaches the universal law of impermanence *that nothing lasts forever and we should be in the "now" to experience that pain or joy, rather than fretting about the joy going away or the pain lasting forever. Our American society battles impermanence at every turn with beauty products to stop our aging and the promise that more "stuff" will lead to happiness. My experience is that embracing these "values," if you can call them that, leads to less happiness, not more. Buddhism's* Four Immeasurable Attitudes (*loving-kindness, compassion, sympathetic joy, and equanimity*) *have helped me deal with unkind people and circumstances and, just as important, bounce back from bad experiences.*

Avoiding fumbles: Boost your resiliency skills and your support network in advance of calamities. Learn *how* to be a better friend to yourself and others when you encounter major setbacks.

Recovering fumbles: Are you depressed because of the death or divorce of a life partner or friend? Has a major health problem surfaced that seems like it will upset, or even end, your fourth quarter? Seek out people who have made it through these life events and recovered well. Ask them how and build a new support network of "club" members (like the Modern

Widows Club or Compassionate Friends) who know what you're experiencing.

Dangers: Difficulty avoiding fumbles. Difficulty bouncing back after a fumble. Diminished happiness. Disagreements with a life partner. Gray divorce. Developing anxiety or depression.

Action plan: Add "Build resiliency skills" to your list of bucket list items for the fourth quarter. Study *how* others have bounced back.

Mars/Venus considerations: There is equal opportunity for fumbles. Men, especially those who get into a "life's not fair" mindset, often have more trouble bouncing back after adversity in the fourth quarter.

Special issues for singles: Resiliency for singles appears to be more difficult for those who have not faced major adversity in their lives. Consider finding a "circle," a small group of people that you feel safe to talk to and can help by sharing their own stories and how they are facing adversity. Listen to TED talks or read books about other singles who faced difficult times and made it through to a better place.

Kaizen (small steps to success) ideas: Ask one friend who has gone through a tough time how he or she is doing. Ask questions and don't be afraid your friend will be offended. Your friend will likely be more offended if you appear more self-absorbed in your own problems instead of his or her issues.

More Help

Other potential mistakes related to **decision** fumbles, available at www.FourthQuartersFumbles.com:

- **"If Only" Regrets** – spending too much time ruminating over what could have been better in your life, versus making the future better.

"Making Better Decisions" Worksheet

Personal assessment: Rate the following statements from 1 to 5:

1 = this statement doesn't describe me

5 = this statement is exactly like me

"I know how to make good decisions."

Rating: 1   2   3   4   5

Personal assessment: Rate the following statements from 1 to 5:

"I regularly follow up on my decisions."

Rating: 1   2   3   4   5

Personal assessment: Rate the following statements from 1 to 5:

"I'm good at bouncing back from adversity."

Rating: 1   2   3   4   5

The one person in my life who makes good decisions, follows through and bounces back well is: _____

_____

My plan for making better decisions and building future resiliency is: _____

_____

My one Kaizen (small step to success) step will be: _____

_____

CHAPTER 4

Having a Good Transition Plan

The best laid plans of mice and men often go awry.

– adapted from Robert Burns

A transition plan is different than a financial plan. The best transition plans can be very simple. It should be uniquely suited to you and your personality and goals. It should be top of mind at all times so when you encounter inevitable challenges, you have a "true north star" to guide you.

Potential Red-Zone Fumble #3: Not Asking the Right Questions About the Future

Have you considered some of the questions raised earlier as you approached the fourth quarter? Do you know what your *Why?* is, or *Who* you're going to hang around with in the fourth quarter? Do you have a sense of *Where* you want to live at various stages of the fourth quarter?

Avoiding fumbles: Ask the right questions. If you're married, do this together with your spouse or life partner, or do it separately and then compare the results. If you're single, do this with a close friend. Discuss your answers with close friends, family, and your financial planner to get good reality checks on your answers.

- What am I going to do with more free time? *Usually answered by a mix of How Much?, Why?, Who? and Where?*

- Does my circle of friends include the right people to hang around as I age? *The important Who? question.*

- If I'm going to have more time than my parents in the fourth quarter, do I need an "encore" career, paid or unpaid? What should I do that will make me happy in that career and will also leave time for other pursuits? *Sometimes dictated by the How Much? answers and part of having a satisfying Why? later in life.*

- Are we happy in our current home or hometown? Should we consider a move or downsize in stage 1 (the go-go years) of the fourth quarter or should we wait until later to see where children and grandchildren will be living? *Your How Much? and Where? questions at different points in the fourth quarter.*

- What will I do every day of the week? *Your Why? and your Who?* (See the sample questionnaire in Appendix 4).

- Where do I want to travel with my spouse or life partner? *Part of the Where? equation.*

- Where do I want to travel alone or with my best friends? How will my life partner feel about that? *Important Who? questions.*
- What do I want to learn to keep myself sharp, fresh, and interesting? *This helps your Why? and your Who?*

Recovering fumbles: It's not unusual for people in stage 1 of the fourth quarter to fumble in their transition planning, recover, and try again. It's dangerous when they fumble and never recover, usually leading to a slow decline into depression with multiple mistakes leading from the first one. It can also be dangerous to have regrets later in life about what you didn't do.

Dangers: Losing momentum in the go-go years. Creating problems with a life partner. Having friends or family question your priorities, creating stress fractures.

Action plan: When you and your life partner are on the same page with your transition plan, take action towards those goals. When you get it wrong, determine if it takes adjustment or if you need to try something different. Was it your *How?* that malfunctioned instead of your *What?* Your financial planner can help you evaluate transition cash-flow scenarios and implementation ideas for the action plan.

Mars/Venus considerations: Men often struggle more with transition plans. Career women who feel they need to work longer to make up for lost years raising children occasionally find they experience the same problems.

Special issues for singles: Not having a significant other to bounce ideas around with for the fourth quarter can make transition planning harder. On the other hand, you may have less baggage from someone with very different views or values to contend with. Consider freedom a gift. Many single women move to a group-living retirement community earlier (some in their early 70s) to enhance their sense of community and find opportunities to date.

Kaizen (small steps to success) ideas: Jot down a few ideas of your *Why?*, your *Who?* and your *Where?* in the next stage of your life.

Potential Red-Zone Fumble #4:
Values Alignment Failure

If your transition plan, or any of the moves you make in the fourth quarter, doesn't align with your values, you increase your chance of failure. It could be failure to live up to your own expectations (leading to deep regrets later on) or failure to live up to your life partner or children's expectations. Strong values and being in touch with those values often sets the tone for the *How?* in going about decision making and follow through.

> *It's practically impossible to have razor-sharp decision skills and strong resilience skills without a clear sense of your own values and your family values.*

Avoiding fumbles: Be clear going into the fourth quarter about your values and those of your life partner. Where are they the same and where do they differ? When you have key decisions to make, be very mindful of your values as you consider options. Often what seems like a very tough decision becomes relatively easy when values are used as the first criteria in decision-making.

Recovering fumbles: A major values misfire on your part can be hard to recover from, especially if it has created a rift in the family. Admitting your role in creating the problem, rather than defending the decision with gusto, will go a long way in getting back on the right track with those around you.

If a life partner or family member has a lapse in judgement, lend an ear or a helping hand rather than being judgmental. All too often seniors become more judgmental as they age, making it difficult to be around them and even harder to stomach when they tell you, "I told you so."

It is also common for people to lose track of their values during their working life or not have them well aligned. Sometimes values in a career have been set aside in favor of making money.

> *The fourth quarter is a marvelous opportunity to realign your values with your life.*

Dangers: Poor decision making. Deep regrets. Family disagreements. Gray divorce. Developing anxiety or depression.

Action plan: Get aligned with your values as you develop or refine your transition plan. Use the values assessment in the appendix with your life partner and spend time discussing what each area means. Set the tone for your *How?*

Mars/Venus considerations: Values misalignment is more prevalent in men, but we have seen many women (working and not) have challenges in this area.

Special issues for singles: Singles interviewed for this book suggest that values are even more important for them to maintain a "true north," get where you want to go approach to life. Different values often present problems with siblings making decisions about elderly parents and a host of other fumble areas.

Kaizen (small steps to success) ideas: Write down your top three values. How do they potentially impact your *How Much?*, your *Why?*, your *Who?*, your *Where?* and your *How?*

More Help

Other potential mistakes related to **transition** fumbles, available at www.FourthQuartersFumbles.com:

- **Life Partners at Different Stages** – aging at different rates or stopping working at different times can create challenges. We've seen some fourth quarter couples turn these dangers into strengths.

- **A Stale Transition Plan** – occasionally people find their initial *Why?* or *Who?* or *Where?* strategies aren't working well. Perhaps they have these figured out but are misfiring on the *How?* Learn how to adapt and pivot better.

"Better Transition Plan" Worksheet

Personal assessment: Rate the following statements from 1 to 5:
1 = this statement doesn't describe me
5 = this statement is exactly like me

"I have a good transition plan into the fourth quarter."
Rating: 1   2   3   4   5

Personal assessment: Rate the following statements from 1 to 5:

"I'm following through well on my transition plan."
Rating: 1   2   3   4   5

Personal assessment: Rate the following statements from 1 to 5:

"I know my core values."
Rating: 1   2   3   4   5

My greatest transition plan challenges may be: _____
_____

The one person in my life who has done the best job of transitioning in various life stages is: _____
_____

My one Kaizen (small step to success) step will be: _____
_____

CHAPTER 5

A Balanced Financial and Investment Strategy

Money won't make you happy, but neither will poverty.

— Warren Buffett

There are ample financial planning and investment opportunities for fumbles in the go-go, slow-go, and no-go stages of the fourth quarter. A question that keeps coming up at meetings of top advisors that I attend or speak at is whether the *real* threats or the *imagined* threats are more dangerous these days?

The real threats include the playbook being different for those entering the fourth quarter. In the "old days," 60% stocks and 40% cash and fixed income (usually bonds) was the gold standard for investing success. Study after study reinforced this balance as being optimal as retirees began to withdraw money from portfolios. Today, changes in the risk-reward characteristics of bonds and stocks makes this playbook less ideal for many investors.

The imagined threats are every bit as dangerous and fall under the category of "behavioral landmines." Fear and greed remain the primary emotions that can cause investors to shift their strategy at the wrong time and create fourth quarter fumbles. The relentless 24/7 media machine can magnify these emotions. For the fourth quarter, fear creating bad decisions is the greater risk.

Although your professional support team (which may include an attorney, financial advisor, financial planner, CPA and/or insurance agent) can help you at each stage deal with real and imagined threats, it's good to consider in advance where specific fumbles might occur.

Potential Red-Zone Fumble #5: Investing Without a Well-Thought-Out Plan

All too often, retirees spend less time preparing for the stage-1 go-go years of the fourth quarter than they do researching a vacation or new car purchase. It pays to be more intentional and develop a strong vision for at least the next 3 to 5 years of stage-1 living.

Avoiding fumbles: Developing a future financial vision that matches your living expenses with your portfolio cash flow and returns is a good step towards understanding the appropriate investment allocation for you and your situation. *Well-thought-out* means doing some visualization of how your lifestyle will be different and how that could affect cash flow. Note that a good transition plan is a very helpful step to creating a solid foundation for the future financial vision.

Recovering fumbles: In today's rapidly changing world it's not unusual that fourth quarter investors find that their portfolios aren't matching their needs, the investment environment, or their ability to tolerate risk now that they are not receiving a paycheck anymore. Consult professionals and consider small course corrections rather than major changes, unless it's clear you've had poor advice up to this point and need a major overhaul coming into the fourth quarter.

Dangers: Cash-flow problems. Portfolio hazards. Disagreements with a life partner. Gray divorce. Developing anxiety or depression.

Action plan: Update or develop a well-thought out retirement cash flow plan. Update the plan at least every 3 to 5 years.

Mars/Venus considerations: Equal potential for fumbles.

Special issues for singles: Same potential for fumbles, although some singles perceive a need to have even more financial safety margins in their non-working years. These fears are rarely as real or dangerous as they feel, but again the "one size fits one" fourth quarter reality means considering more carefully how the future will unfold.

Kaizen (small steps to success) ideas: Know where your cash is coming from and going.

Potential Red Zone Fumble #6:
Not Considering the Extra Cash Flow Needed

If you've already developed a good transition plan, especially the *Why?* and the *Who?*, it may have already occurred to you that there is more opportunity to spend money when you're not working. This ranges from eating out more frequently to having more free time to spend money on travel and hobbies.

The first year or two of true retirement is a good test of cash-flow needs. If you're like many who have a staged cash flow in retirement as a result of staggered payouts or part-time consulting, you may need to keep track of expenses to have a real sense of what you're going to need to live comfortably throughout the fourth quarter.

It's not unusual to spend more in your go-go years, including bigger trips that may double (or more) your travel budget in the first 5 to 10 years of fewer or no work commitments. It's fine to splurge as long as you've considered these extra expenses in your financial planning and identify expenses you may not have considered. These can include children who need special financial assistance, special trips with your family, educational/health needs of grandchildren, and health expenses not covered under Medicare or your Medicare supplement plan.

> **Avoiding fumbles:** In the first year of living more from your portfolio than your paycheck (semiretirement or full retirement), you may be amazed at how much extra you spend. Keeping a monthly budget can help track your actual versus targeted expenses. Depending on how much of a margin of safety you determined you have in your future cash flow plan, you can then decide how budget overruns should be handled.

> **Recovering fumbles:** Spending too much is dangerous for some individuals who may leave fewer resources for the stage 2 slow-go years. If you know you're spending too much *and* you

know (rather than suspect) this is dangerous to your long-term financial health, consider trimming some areas.

If you're trimming expenses just because your DNA is conservative or you're worried about investment markets or world events, you face the danger of missing out on experiences while you have the health to enjoy them. Your spouse or life partner may take a dim view of this trade-off if you don't at least discuss the pros and cons with him or her one-on-one or in conjunction with your financial planner.

Dangers: Cash-flow problems. Portfolio hazards. Disagreements with a life partner. Gray divorce. Developing anxiety or depression.

Action plan: Know what you're spending. Put it in the context of a plan and a knowledge of safety margins given your unique set of facts. *How* would you adjust spending if you needed to?

Mars/Venus considerations: Early in the fourth quarter, we often hear from men that they believe they will die early and that they want to "make hay while the sun shines," spending more sooner in the go-go years. Later in the fourth quarter, men seem to have a tendency to tighten up too much on spending.

Special issues for singles: Same potential for fumbles.

Kaizen (small steps to success) ideas: If you're trimming "want" item expenses like the latest, greatest smart enabled TV, discuss which one to trim first with your life partner. No life partner? Discuss with your financial planner.

Potential Red-Zone Fumble #7:
Waiting Too Long for Financial Help

Many do-it-yourselfers and validators (who get spot advice from professionals but mostly do their own investing and planning) do fine well into the first go-go stage of the fourth quarter but then begin a slow fumbling process as their desire, ability or time to keep up with financial matters wanes. One solution is to have a trusted professional financial advisor designated as a backup to investors who believe they will know when it's time to turn over the financial reins to someone else. Reality has often turned out somewhat different. As financial acumen declines over time, so does awareness of the need for help.

Those who enter the 5-year "warning track" to dementia (see the chart in chapter 1) find that chemical changes in their brain often short-circuit their ability to make good decisions.

Avoiding fumbles: Set up a system where a trusted friend, life partner, spouse, or professional advisor will feel comfortable letting you know when it's time to delegate financial authority. The first warning sign is often erratic behavior (being more inclined to listen to a doom-and-gloom salesperson or selling assets in a downturn) or the inability to balance a checkbook.

Recovering fumbles: Early on in the fumble cycle, mistakes can often be remedied with decisive action. Do what is right for your situation and family, even though you might be admitting you made some mistakes.

Dangers: Reduced investment returns. A rudderless financial ship. Disagreements with a life partner.

Action plan: Your *how* here is critical. Have a back-up financial plan that has a good chance of actually working when the time comes. Keep good records so someone taking over knows *where* everything is located and *why* some decisions have been made. Determine in advance *who* will help you with financial matters. If you're concerned about having one advisor, have a back-up advisor (like a CPA) be a watchdog for some period of time.

The moment you or anyone around you detects signs of possible dementia, take action. Get a cognitive test locally or at a well-known clinic such as Cooper, Duke, or Mayo. Don't be the Queen or King of De-Nile.

Mars/Venus considerations: Men are more likely to try to keep control for too long in the fourth quarter.

Special issues for singles: More dangerous since you may not recognize the signs of slippage and begin making crucial investing mistakes.

Kaizen (small steps to success) ideas: Have at least one trusted friend or advisor who you discuss financial matters with and who can give you common-sense direction.

Potential Red-Zone Fumble #8: Bait and Switch and Other Schemes and Scams

There are many hucksters selling "retire comfortably" snake oil in the marketplace. Some are outright scams or frauds (like Bernie Madoff), and some are promoting benefits that are unlikely to come true. The old adage, "If it looks too good to be true, it probably is," should be remembered at all times.

Most prevalent in today's market are annuities that "guarantee" 6 or 7% rates of return. However, just try to cash them in 5 or 10 years from now and get that return. Instead, the return is only available if you trade your equity for a lifetime stream of income at return rates that are usually below average or below market. During the holding period, annual fees of 2 to 4% are common. The insurance companies giveth and then they taketh away. If you've fallen for one of these pitches, it may not result in an outright fumble. Instead, you may have just created an asset with subpar returns that should be treated as part of your "short-term bond" allocation.

Another troubling type of annuity provides a lower guaranteed return and a percentage of the gains in the stock market each year. Since stock returns tend to be "lumpy" (larger returns lumped into a few years out of every 10, instead of a high average return), these index annuities have generally not performed as advertised for consumers. In one case we analyzed, a 10-year return in what was supposed to be a 70% stock and 30% bond portfolio turned out to resemble a 70% bond and 30% stock portfolio. The unfortunate purchasers of this annuity had lost a large chunk of their stage 1 go-go retirement money growth and were unable to afford the continuing-care retirement community that they had hoped to live in someday.

Some years back I was part of a statewide aging initiative that included many different entities and leaders in the "better aging" movement. The briefing we had from the state attorney general and his staff on scams being perpetrated every day on seniors was appalling. Isolated seniors were targeted more frequently for these scams.

Avoiding fumbles: Always "sleep on" decisions to buy assets you've just learned about. Run them by at least one of your advisors and get an independent opinion.

Recovering fumbles: If you've bought something you find out later you shouldn't have, seek advice from professionals on the best way to remedy the situation. True scams should be reported to law enforcement authorities or your state's attorney general.

Dangers: Reduced investment returns. Life partner disagreements. Major life disappointments as dreams become less affordable.

Action plan: Be an informed consumer. Consult trusted advisors.

Mars/Venus considerations: Equal opportunities for fumbles.

Special issues for singles: Single women are often a target because of the perception they are more vulnerable. Be prepared, "appropriately paranoid" and use the cautions discussed above.

Kaizen (small steps to success) ideas: Read an article or two from trusted sources when considering an investment.

More Help

Other potential mistakes related to **financial** fumbles, available at www.FourthQuartersFumbles.com:

- **Penny Wise, Pound Foolish** – balancing spending for the here and now, and saving for the future, remains a lifelong challenge!

- **Investing Too Conservatively** – in a time of low returns on conservative assets, we've found that many future plans can fail by being too safety minded.

- **Taxing Dilemma** – the delicate balance between being tax efficient and not letting the tax tail wag the financial dog.

- **Investing for Cash Flow Only** – an attempt to get back to the "old school" approach of living off investment income. In today's very different interest rate and economic environment, this approach still has merit but dangers to consider that weren't around in the "old days."

"Balanced Financial and Investment Strategy" Worksheet

Personal assessment: Rate the following statements from 1 to 5:

1 = this statement doesn't describe me

5 = this statement is exactly like me

"I have a well thought out financial plan."

Rating: 1   2   3   4   5

Personal assessment: Rate the following statements from 1 to 5:

*"I know my spending patterns
and how the future may impact my spending."*

Rating: 1   2   3   4   5

Personal assessment: Rate the following statements from 1 to 5:

*"I'm concerned that my emotions
will cause bad financial decisions in the future."*

Rating: 1   2   3   4   5

Who do you know who makes consistently good financial decisions? _____

_____

Who is the one person you trust the most in your financial matters: _____

_____

My one Kaizen (small step to success) step will be: _____

_____

CHAPTER 6

Having a Good
Reason to Get Out of Bed

Too many people die with their music still in them.

– Oliver Wendell Holmes

My experience and dozens of aging experts interviewed for this book suggest that not having a good *Why?*, a reason to get out of bed in the morning, will create significant emotional and financial problems throughout the fourth quarter. A Harvard study clearly showed that boredom is a high predictor of a lousy fourth quarter experience. The findings of the study also indicated that lack of interest in bettering one's self, engaging with family, and staying healthy will very likely lead to many fourth quarter fumbles, including anxiety, depression, financial missteps, and poor decision-making into stage 2 and stage 3 of the fourth quarter.

Find a good *Why?*, and chances are you'll find more fun in the fourth quarter, and be more fun to be around, helping out your *Who?* Interesting people like to be around interesting people who have a positive outlook on life.

As referenced previously, many have discovered their optimum *Why?* only to be foiled by the *How?*, not figuring out *how* to best implement the *Why?*

Elaine in Colorado, who we heard from in the first chapter, is 79 years old and was an early retiree in her 50s with her husband, Win. Elaine is a gerontologist by training and she coauthored a *Successful Aging* training guide for hospital systems, caregivers, and care centers. Elaine embarked on an extended fourth quarter with gusto. She stayed well engaged with many mind and body pursuits throughout the go-go years, including travelling with her husband and with girlfriends. She had always wanted to learn to oil paint but had never gotten around to it. Finally, at age 78, following up on her theme of, "If not now, when?" she decided there was no time like the present.

"My experience with painting has been a lot of hard work learning brushstrokes and techniques used by good painters, says Elaine. "After a dedicated month of classes and practice, I just sold 5 paintings in a local art show. It was satisfying to be recognized by others, but mostly I'm proud of myself for not losing that dream."

Elaine gained more than just a new hobby that scratched her itch for creativity. She continued, "By chance, the author of a book on the 'power of experiencing awe-inspiring events' was in town for a book signing. A reporter interviewed me for the event since it was the awe of the beauty of the wilderness that inspired my best paintings. Suddenly I realized I had yet another reason to keep myself young in spirit and body – I still have adventures to go on and important family milestones to watch and admire."

Potential Red-Zone Fumble #9: Getting Into a Comfortable Routine Without Intentionality

It is easy in the stage 1 "go-go" years of the fourth quarter to get overly comfortable, especially if you were in a high-stress job and needed significant decompression to get back into healthy mental and physical shape.

> **Avoiding fumbles:** Explore different consulting options that utilize your past skills and experience (going cold turkey from a career can be stressful for some people), consider different ways to give back to your community or favorite social cause, and identify existing and new hobbies to maintain a good sense of challenge and fun. If you're not feeling challenged to continue learning and growing, look for other opportunities.

> **Recovering fumbles:** We've seen plenty of situations where an individual has an initial game plan, gets comfortable in a new routine, and then forgets when to change the plan. Or they have the plan changed by outside forces and they don't actively adjust.

Dangers: Boredom. Disagreements with a life partner. Gray divorce. Developing anxiety or depression.

Action plan: Ask yourself every day or every week, "Am I doing what makes me happy and keeps me sharp and engaged with life?" Pay attention to life partners or friends who suggest you're not using yourself to full potential. Figure out the *how*.

Mars/Venus considerations: Both genders can fall victim to this fumble, often in different ways.

Special issues for singles: Greater opportunity for fumbles in some cases where underconfidence or anxiety creates inertia.

Kaizen (small steps to success) ideas: Overcome inertia by exploring a resource (talk with one well-connected person, consult one of the website's listed in the Resource section of the Appendix) that helps you consider "encore" fourth quarter opportunities.

Potential Red-Zone Fumble #10: Losing Your Attitude of Gratitude

Happiness experts have long known through studying cultures in the U.S. and around the world that chasing happiness can be a frustrating experience. For some it always seems just out of reach. For others it is, "I'll be happy when [fill-in the blank]": I've reached the top of my profession. I've got the home and car I've always wanted. I have children. I get my children out of college. I'm financially independent.

Chris, a recently retired active 70-year-old, was a prominent manager of ski resorts around the country and the recent author of *Ski Inc: My Journey through Four Decades in the Ski-Resort Business, from the Founding Entrepreneurs to Mega-Companies*. He told me the tale of an early ski resort in Killington, Vermont. The resort had poor equipment; made poor snow when needed; gave people a short, mediocre experience; and yet people were grateful for just being able to ski. Fast forward to great equipment, technology, and wonderful conditions and yet more people complain today than ever before. What happened?

The expectations bar shifted. We now have more forms of entertainment. As a result of world-class travel experiences through professional managers like Disney, our sense of what is acceptable has shifted so we're less grateful for what we believe is a mediocre experience.

Here is the *how*: you can be grateful for small things and big things. Happiness experts note that gratitude for "things" is much more fleeting than gratitude for friends, family, and experiences such as travelling to new places with people we care about or watching a perfect sunset.

Avoiding fumbles: Be conscious every day about what you are grateful for. If you believe in a higher power, tell that power but also tell the people you're grateful for on a regular basis. Don't assume that "they just know."

Recovering fumbles: If you've slid into a place where you find yourself complaining about people, politics, your health, your family, or a host of other things, write down what you have to be grateful for and put the list on the refrigerator. If you're a perfectionist and nothing measures up to "good enough," don't cross "pretty good" people and experiences off the list.

Dangers: Disagreements with a life partner. Gray divorce. Developing anxiety or depression.

Action plan: Reframe your mind-set. Look for the good.

Mars/Venus considerations: Men tend to lose their attitude of gratitude more than women, often because they had too much of their sense of self invested in their careers and find the fourth quarter less stimulating and satisfying than they imagined.

Special issues for singles: Equal opportunity for fumbles.

Kaizen (small steps to success) ideas: For one day, write down the three things you have to be grateful for at the end of the day. Thank the people you meet every opportunity you get. Tell at least one person that day why you treasure them.

Special stage-of-life issues:

Stage 1 (go-go): Critical to getting the fourth quarter off to a good start and keeping your attitude level positive and forward-looking.

Stage 2 (slow-go): Critical to make it through the inevitable health problems that occur more frequently in this stage.

Stage 3 (no-go): Having just visited a long-time client and friend in the hospital on what could have been his last days, I noticed an attitude of being grateful for what he had accomplished, what he had experienced, the people who loved him, and the legacy he had taken time to build for the future. His doctor remarked that his good humor in the face of losing the battle of aging was inspiring. It was no surprise to his doctors when he recovered to watch one more sunset and hold his wife and family one more time.

Potential Red-Zone Fumble #11:
Letting a Life Setback Derail Your Purpose

Many tests of your resiliency are normal in the fourth quarter. An all-too-frequent occurrence that causes fourth quarter fumbles is when an inevitable setback causes you to change your routine and lose momentum in areas of physical, mental, and spiritual growth. It could be slipping and falling, followed by months of rehab. It could be a family crisis that requires you to care for a family member. Or it could be an external event that deeply disturbs you, ranging from a perceived or real change in cultural attitudes in your family, to changes in the world in general.

We've often heard the refrain, "The world is just so different from what it used to be. I don't know how to keep up or fit in."

Avoiding fumbles: Sharpen your resiliency skills before you need them. Stay focused on your own unique "true north." Guide back (often with the help of family and true friends) to your course after the crisis passes, determine to press through, and continue with your lifelong learning-and-improvement plan.

Read the book *Option B: Facing Adversity, Finding Resilience, and Building Joy* by Sheryl Sandberg and Adam Grant.

Recovering fumbles: Check in at regular intervals on your transition plan and wheel of life. Are you losing steam in multiple areas and can't seem to find the will to get back on your desired course? Consider this your number-one challenge and top priority. You won't be any help to your life partner or family members if you become part of the problem instead of part of the solution. Find the will and your way back, with some help from friends, family, a life coach, your financial planner, a mental-health therapist, or clergy.

Dangers: Disagreements with a life partner. Family conflict. Gray divorce. Developing anxiety or depression.

Action plan: Resolve today to understand how to bounce back better and help friends and family bounce back.

Mars/Venus considerations: Both men and women are subject to this fumble.

Special issues for singles: Dangerous for singles if they don't have ingrained bounce-back skills already and are not surrounded by a strong social network.

Kaizen (small steps to success) ideas: Read one article or one book on people who bounced back from adversity.

More Help

Other potential mistakes related to **Getting-Out-of-Bed** fumbles, available at www.FourthQuartersFumbles.com:

- **Mistaking a Bucket List for a Life Engagement List** – Many get too engaged in their own bucket list and ignore their family and friends, with predictable consequences.

"Getting-out-of-Bed" Worksheet

Personal assessment: Rate the following statements from 1 to 5:

 1 = this statement doesn't describe me

 5 = this statement is exactly like me

"I know my Why? in life."

Rating: 1   2   3   4   5

Personal assessment: Rate the following statements from 1 to 5:

"I'm living my Why? in line with my core values."

Rating: 1   2   3   4   5

Who is the one person in my life who best exemplifies matching their *why* and their values? _____

_____

My one Kaizen (small step to success) step will be: _____

_____

CHAPTER 7

Wellness versus
the Absence of Illness

To lengthen thy life, lessen thy meals.

— Benjamin Franklin

Benjamin Franklin had a number of his best achievements in the fourth quarter, and given life expectancy in his day, he went into "overtime" in the game of life. He was a man of many talents: scientist, inventor/innovator, diplomat, writer, musician, postmaster, founding father, and fitness guru. Fitness guru? Wiser than Dr. Oz, less annoying than Richard Simmons. He was long-lived like Jack Lalanne. Franklin was touting proper diet and advocating exercise over two centuries before it became fashionable.

Let's revisit the 2016 EBRI study results from chapter 1: "80% of healthy respondents were "very satisfied" after 15 years of retirement, compared to 25% who were in poor health." This gap in satisfaction levels is remarkable. Good health is our number-one asset, and like all assets, we can nurture it and have a better chance of maintaining wellness deep into the fourth quarter. There is also the random chance that something in our bodies will malfunction. With the advances coming in medical science, I'd rather pursue wellness and perhaps live long enough that they will figure out how to fix whatever ends up threatening to sound the buzzer on my fourth quarter of life.

Franklin, then in his seventies, living in Paris, let himself go eating rich food and exercising less frequently. For most of his life, he was a prime physical specimen. Biographer Walter Isaacson described him as muscular, barrel-chested, and almost six feet tall.

Franklin's fascination with fitness began at the young age of 17. Working as a typesetter in London, he garnered respectable physical prowess by running up and down stairs with heavy trays of lead type. Often, he would carry two trays instead of one, a feat that wowed his colleagues. At the same time, he eschewed drinking alcohol, choosing water instead, and convinced his coworkers to do the same.

Here is a letter from Franklin to a friend late in life that well describes the balance of challenges that occur late in the fourth quarter along with the intermittent good times:

You kindly enquire after my Health. I have not of late much reason to boast of it. People that will live a long Life and drink to the Bottom of the Cup expect to meet with some of the Dregs. However, when I consider how many more terrible maladies the human Body is liable to, I think my self well off that I have only three incurable ones, the Gout, the Stone, and Old Age; and, those notwithstanding, I enjoy many comfortable Intervals, in which I forget all my Ills, and amuse myself in Reading or Writing, or in Conversation with Friends, joking, laughing, and telling merry Stories, as when you first knew me, a young Man about Fifty.

How many considered themselves young at age 50 in the 1700s? How many of us today still consider ourselves young at age 50?

In this discussion of health, I distinguish between the absence of illness (no major health issues or chronic problems being treated) and wellness, where you actually feel better than you would if you weren't doing the right things for your mind, body, and spirit. Modern medicine has focused a lot on the absence of illness. That's important, because pain of any magnitude can make it hard for you to enjoy simple pleasures or travel or a host of other fourth quarter activities.

Your body is a complex machine tied directly to your brain. Get the chemistry off kilter and you may find yourself snapping at a loved one or being difficult to be around. Don't be surprised if your life partner decides to leave you permanently late in the game, a growing phenomenon in America.

Wellness matters! All the money in the world often can't buy happiness and certainly can't always ensure good health even with the best medical care available. A few simple things done every day have been shown to lower the potential for health-care fumbles and create a higher quality of life deeper into the fourth quarter. These are:

Eat sensibly. You don't need to adhere to the perfect diet all the time, just follow a diet that focuses on moderation in portions and intake of sugars and bad fats. Will eating even better create wellness and extend the quantity and quality of your life even more? Probably, but there are many factors in play including family history.

Exercise your body regularly. Like your diet, your exercise regimen doesn't have to be relentless, with workouts every day. Exercise experts for seniors believe that you can achieve a high percentage of absence-of-illness benefits by just walking for 20 minutes three times a week. For wellness, doing more can be beneficial to your heart and weight as long as it's in moderation. The *Younger Next Year* authors suggest a 6-day-a-week exercise program with at least four aerobic fitness days.

Get enough sleep. A variety of causes can interrupt sleep in the fourth quarter. Recent studies suggest this is a recipe for many bad decisions and being grumpy on a regular basis, followed by blowing off your exercise program. Then the long and occasionally painful drop down the waterfall begins. The Human Sleep Science center at Berkley has even determined causal links to inadequate sleep and the onset of dementia and Alzheimer's.

Exercise your brain regularly. Opportunities can range from reading a new book every week or two (on diverse topics), doing crossword puzzles, playing Mahjong or bridge, or engaging in thoughtful conversations with friends or strangers.

Some seniors take this a step further and enroll in university courses, even learning a new language deep in the fourth quarter. There is some evidence this will lead to better wellness and possibly stave off the onset of certain brain disorders deeper into the fourth quarter.

Feed your spirit. Regardless of your religious or spiritual beliefs, it has been shown time and again that healthy aging deep into the fourth quarter benefits from a good spiritual foundation, and many people need a belief in some higher power beyond the mortal plane of existence. Yet for some, this is precisely the time of their life when they may question their spiritual beliefs. Even ministers, rabbis, and shamans have times when they question their faith. They turn to others to help them through these rough patches. Avoid fumbles by having a spiritual social network in addition to your other friends and family.

These are important basics. Michael Jordan famously said mastering the basics is the foundation for all great success. **How you master the basics is important.** Unless you have fabulous DNA and lots of luck, it is doubtful you will have a great fourth quarter without some measure of the basics. That's why I go every year to the famed Cooper Clinic in Dallas. Named one of the top destinations for a comprehensive physical by Fortune and Worth magazines, it has helped many of my childhood heroes, from presidents to astronauts to Noble laureates, who wanted to increase their odds of better health results in the fourth quarter.

Beyond the basics, there are other things you can do to pursue the pinnacle of wellness.

Experience has taught me that an obsession with any of the following areas may cause fumbles in other areas of your life, so be mindful about how much time, focus, and energy you use in these areas.

Examples include:

- Completing bucket-list items you've always wanted to do that involve exercising your body or brain

- Pursuing higher spiritual learning at home or around the world

- Developing entirely new pursuits that take you back to the "beginners mind," a place that was intriguing and perhaps exhilarating earlier in life. In the fourth quarter, "intriguing" may become "frustrating" without the right frame of mind. I've found that living through the fourth quarter experiences of clients and reading different views of the fourth quarter achievements and frustrations of historical figures – including Benjamin Franklin – have helped me prepare for my own challenges in the future.

- Tackling a major legacy project that will live on and create positive impact for the world long after you depart

There are cities around the country that have just the right mix of these ingredients to foster wellness. Consider these options carefully. Simple things such as being able to walk without discomfort from weather (hot or cold) can extend your health and well-being. Being around like-minded people can also be a good motivator to keep your health at a better level as you age.

Want to know more? Read *The Body Builders: Inside the Science of the Engineered Human* by Adam Piore. This book combines vivid storytelling with groundbreaking science to give you a glimpse into what the future may hold from medical science for repairing our bodies.

Potential Red-Zone Fumble #12: Coordinating Health Care

Today's health-care technology and knowledge is the best it's ever been. However, the health-care system is in a state of flux and is often difficult to navigate.

One of our clients was having problems that couldn't be diagnosed. This person went to a different health-care provider and had an in-depth discussion. It turned out that several prescribed drugs were having bad interactions. The regimen was changed, with one of the medications eliminated, and our client was soon feeling much better and playing golf the next week.

Another client had a series of misdiagnoses by seemingly respected practitioners. Bouncing from doctor to specialist for two years, this person finally had a day-long intensive physical at a respected clinic. The mystery was solved, the new treatment worked, and the client returned to the fourth quarter plan, but not without the loss of considerable time and momentum, not to mention the "cost" of being in chronic pain for two years longer than necessary.

Avoiding fumbles: Choose your health-care providers carefully. Are they proactive or reactive? Do they go the extra mile to figure out your unique problem? Is your primary-care physician just coasting towards retirement or staying on top of their game?

If you have good financial resources, consider a *health care concierge*. These are doctors who have disconnected from the regular medical system. You pay an annual fee (usually $5,000 to $20,000) and get more personalized facetime with a physician than in the normal doctor checkup. I've also seen a few good hybrid concierge models that still help coordinate health insurance but give you more facetime with nurses, physicians assistants and physicians. The caveat here is just as with other areas of life, there are aces and jokers in concierge medicine. Interview a few, ask for references and choose wisely.

A relatively new category of health-care advocate is a *health-care navigator*. People in this role are often employed by major hospitals or health-care systems to assist in navigating complex healthcare options. The usual caveat: if you don't feel you're getting the right advice, keep searching.

Ask a friend or family member to be your *health-care advocate*. Common sense and good listening skills are higher skill priorities than a health-care degree for your advocate. An advocate accompanies you to meetings with doctors and specialists and may hear and see important things you do not.

Recovering fumbles: Not getting the right result from your health-care choices? Pursue a second opinion. If you think your primary health-care system is failing you, chose another path. Consult with friends and your social network for options and a referral. See if there is a health-care navigator in your area.

Dangers: Disagreements with a life partner. Poor health-care choices. Becoming defocused on important fourth quarter priorities.

Action plan: Consider your health your greatest asset and treat it accordingly. Get an advocate who can truly help and have that person ready before a crisis hits. An annual physical through a comprehensive screening clinic such as the Cooper Clinic can be one of your best investments for the future.

Choose your local health-care providers carefully. Do everything in your power (diet, exercise, etc.) to stay out of the health-care system.

Mars/Venus considerations: Men and women have equal challenges here, although women are more likely to consider having a health-care advocate.

Special issues for singles: Often more challenging for singles. If a family member can't help, find a friend to be your advocate and go with you to important doctor meetings.

Kaizen (small steps to success) ideas: Read one article on how to navigate the health-care system better. Share it with your best friend. Talk about it. (See the references in Appendix 5 for ideas.)

Potential Red-Zone Fumble #13: Poor Diet Habits

As many fourth quarter elders can attest, eating right when you have more time on your hands, more socialization with friends and family, and more travel can be very hard to do. Combine this with the extra boost we get from eating sugar and high-calorie foods and our slowing metabolism in the fourth quarter. It's a recipe that all the exercise in the world can't balance out. No exercise plan can compensate for a poor diet or for portions that are too large.

Everything in moderation is something many mothers tell their children; it's true in many fourth quarter areas for health wellness, especially eating right.

Avoiding fumbles: Here are just a few ideas we've heard from our fourth quarter clients who have avoided this fumble:

Eat smaller portions. American restaurant portions are much larger than healthy diets recommend. Split a meal with your partner, or eat only half and box the other half to go.

Write down what you eat. Doing this for at least a week, and perhaps a month, will imbed in your conscious and unconscious mind how many calories and sugars you're consuming. It helps develop good daily habits. Consider smartphone apps like MyFitnessPal, which I like and use every day.

If you have too much time on your hands, find other things to do than sit and snack. Having too much dead time often leads to multiple fumbles, including overeating.

Find healthier snacks. Lots of options here. Some are even tasty and satisfying!

Learn to cook. It's surprising how many fourth quarter people I interviewed have found pleasure in cooking, reduced the amount of bad stuff in what they eat, and found yet another way to maintain weight while also delighting their spouses.

On vacations, especially cruises, its fine to splurge a bit and eat more tasty foods, but agree in advance with your life partner or a friend to help keep your diet balanced.

Moderate your alcohol consumption. Alcohol was consumed in great quantities as our parents entered retirement, creating a multitude of fumbles and health problems. If you don't moderate, be prepared for many fumbles.

Recovering fumbles: If your clothes aren't fitting well after retirement, small adjustments from the list above can get you back into your third quarter wardrobe. Try to figure out, with help from good friends and family, if there is a reason you're eating more and gaining weight. Direct your efforts towards getting more active, including walking every day.

Dangers: There is a growing risk of type 2 diabetes and heart problems, and there is increased risk of other health problems. Other dangers include loss of self-esteem and higher health costs in the fourth quarter, not to mention clothes that don't fit well.

Action plan: Pay attention to diet in the fourth quarter. Resist the urge to eat like a king just because you may have the financial resources of a king. Have regular meetings with a nutrition specialist, ideally one who also is part of an annual physical checkup.

Mars/Venus considerations: Weight gain in the fourth quarter affects men more frequently than women. Men can often gain more benefits from learning to cook than women, who often had the majority of that responsibility during the preceding decades.

Special issues for singles: Equal opportunity for fumbles. Some singles who aren't naturally good at cooking can fall into the trap of eating fast food frequently, a surefire way to create multiple fumbles in the future.

Kaizen (small steps to success) ideas: Cut out one thing for a week. Lowering sugar intake is a great small step.

Potential Red Zone Fumble #14:
Poor Exercise

We know some people who have severely limited their activity in the fourth quarter, usually as a result of anxiety, depression, or becoming a recliner potato, addicted to the constant news reports and binge-watching Netflix or other on-demand TV services. On the other extreme, we know some fourth quarter people who attack exercising like they are training for a marathon. Inevitably they get injured and then swing back to the "too little" side of exercising from the "too much."

People who have made exercise a habit from a young age, as Benjamin Franklin did, often carry these habits into the fourth quarter. Others who have been more sedentary have trouble getting started in the fourth quarter. But we know plenty of people who have simply started a walking routine later in life and kept themselves in good physical shape for many years.

If you want to add 7 years to your lifespan, simply find 20 to 25 minutes for a daily walk. Research presented at the European Society of Cardiology (ESC) Congress followed sixty-nine people between the ages of 30 and 60. Those who engaged in daily moderate exercise, such as a brisk walk or jog, high-intensity interval training (HIIT), and strength training, experienced anti-aging benefits that could add an additional 3 to 7 years to their lives.

The researchers recommended only a 20-minute daily walk to reap the majority of the benefits, which is easy to do and not stressful on joints and muscles. Other studies have suggested a 15-minute walk may be enough. Walking has been found to trigger an anti-aging process and even help repair old DNA.

Study author Sanjay Sharma, professor of inherited cardiac diseases in sports cardiology at St. George's University Hospitals NHS Foundation Trust in London, says, "We may never avoid becoming completely old, but we may delay the time we become old. We may look younger when we're 70 and may live into our nineties. Exercise buys you three to seven additional years of life. It is an antidepressant, it improves cognitive function, and there is now evidence that it may retard the onset of dementia."

Part of what makes walking so beneficial is that when you're walking you can't be *sitting*. Sitting for more than eight hours a day is associated with a 90% increased risk of type 2 diabetes, along with increased risks of heart disease, cancer, and all-cause mortality.

One of The Cooper Institute's (sister organization of the Cooper Clinic) landmark studies found that moderate exercise – a collective 30 minutes of activity most days of the week – will decrease a person's risk of dying from any cause by 58%. Additional research shows that moderate fitness levels will increase a person's lifespan by 6 to 9 years.

A review of 240,000 Cooper Clinic exams on 100,000 patients showed that male patients who regularly get an annual exam live to age 87 – 13 years longer than the average life expectancy for males – and females live to age 90 – 7 years longer.

Need more convincing? Researchers at the University of Colorado found that regular walking helped to prevent peripheral artery disease (which impairs blood flow in the legs and causes leg pain in one-fifth of elderly people). Researchers at the University of Massachusetts medical school found that people who walked every day had 25% fewer colds than those who were sedentary.

Walking can also make you feel good about yourself. A University of Illinois study found that a 20-minute walk at lunchtime, if done for 6 weeks, helps promote good mental health and wellness.

The *Younger Next Year* authors present a compelling case that an aggressive fitness program is your best defense for a host of problems and fumbles in the fourth quarter. I've always been taught that you're like a tomato, either green and growing on the vine or you're dead and rotting on the ground. Pursue growth of mind, body, and spirit. *Younger Next Year* authors Crowley and Lodge walk us through the new biochemistry of aging. They describe our options in a similar way. We're either in a state of growth versus a state of decay, and there isn't much middle ground.

Avoiding fumbles: Several of the expert studies have suggested a gradual increase in activity. Here is one example:

Beginners

- Monday to Saturday: Walk ten minutes at a moderate pace
- Sunday: Walk slowly for 20 minutes

Intermediates

- Monday: Rest
- Tuesday to Friday: Walk for 25 minutes at a moderate pace one day, 30 minutes the next
- Saturday: Walk 20 minutes fast
- Sunday: Walk 45 minutes at a moderate pace

Advanced

- Monday: Rest
- Tuesday to Friday: Walk 45 minutes at a moderate pace one day and 50 minutes the next
- Saturday: Walk 50 minutes at a fast pace
- Sunday: Walk 60 minutes at a moderate pace

If you're also trying to burn fat and get back to your best weight where you feel great and clothes fit, walking somewhat faster (also known as *power walking*) can work, but back off if you feel uncomfortable or have an injury.

Recovering fumbles: We've seen people who get out of their exercise habit, have a number of fumbles and near-fumbles, and then simply get back to walking and rebalance their life. If you've developed a health condition or have an injury preventing you from walking, talk to an exercise coach and your doctor about alternatives. YMCAs around the country have developed a number of "silver sneakers" options to help seniors stay active, and you might even meet some nice people to add to your social network!

Dangers: Declining health. Reduced life expectancy. Less happiness. Weight gain. Developing anxiety or depression.

Action plan: If you like the outdoors, get outside and do something. Too hot or too cold? Look for options. Like to watch TV? Do it on the treadmill. As Nike likes to say, "Just do it."

Mars/Venus considerations: Critical for both men and women.

Special issues for singles: Critical especially if you want to find good companionship in the fourth quarter. We often attract the kind of person we are at the time.

Kaizen (small steps to success) ideas: Take a short walk. Find ways to exercise that you enjoy, including hanging around like-minded people.

Potential Red Zone Fumble #15:
Brain Drain, Depression,
and Sleeping Problems

It is terrible to have a healthy brain trapped inside a deteriorating body. Equally tragic is a healthy body with a deteriorating brain. Some people are good at staying mentally sharp by keeping up with their reading, having stimulating conversations with interesting friends, finding new things to do that stretch their minds and playing mind-exercising games like chess, crossword puzzles, and bridge.

Depression is a growing problem as people in the fourth quarter get bored with themselves, their life partners, their friends, and life in general. If you recognize yourself getting depressed, the answer may be in the chapters on making better decisions (chapter 3), having a good reason to get out of bed (chapter 6), and social networks (chapter 8). If not, you may need some help from your doctor to help create a bridge to a better place.

Nothing will drain the brain as much as poor sleep. Find a solution to poor sleep before it causes untold fumbles in your life.

Avoiding fumbles: Keep a log of daily activities that stretched your brain. Pay special attention to the ones you connected with more deeply. Keep searching for interesting people to hang around with, expanding your social network.

Get enough sleep. Consider comfortable earplugs custom fitted by an ENT physician or Mack's ear plugs, which have saved many marriages in the fourth quarter.

The Human Sleep Science center suggests:

- No alcohol (hard for many in the fourth quarter!) or caffeine in the evening
- A dark room, stay away from TV or computer screens (good thing Johnny Carson isn't on anymore)
- Don't read in bed – train your brain by having a nearby reading chair.
- Keep it cool – 65-68 degrees is recommended.
- Train your brain with regularity. Go to bed at about the same time and get up at about the same time.

Sometimes, simple things may improve our odds of avoiding fumbles. According to a recent longitudinal study at the National University of Singapore, published in *The Journal of Nutrition, Health and Aging,* a cup of tea a day can keep dementia away, and this is especially so for those who are genetically predisposed to the debilitating disease. They discovered that tea drinking reduces the risk of cognitive impairment in older persons by 50 percent and as much as 86 percent (!) for those who are genetically at risk of Alzheimer's. The research team also discovered that the neuroprotective role of tea consumption on cognitive function is not limited to a particular type of tea — so long as the tea is brewed from tea leaves, such as green, black or oolong tea.

Recovering fumbles: If you find yourself getting bored or depressed or are having more trouble keeping up with conversations, get a medical checkup while you double down on your efforts to stay current and sharp.

Be careful of overconfidence; many friendships have been ruined in the fourth quarter as one person became frozen in his or her own belief that one future or one way of doing things was "the only way."

Dangers: Deteriorating relationships. Disagreements with a life partner. Developing anxiety or depression.

Action plan: Be as intentional about keeping your brain sharp as you do with keeping your body in good shape. At the very first sign of your cognitive abilities slipping (often a close friend will be the first to alert you), get a cognitive evaluation done. Major national health-screening programs like the Cooper Clinic can do these as well as specialists in your own hometown.

Mars/Venus considerations: Lack of sleep has been shown to age men by about ten years, with reduced testosterone and energy levels. Men are more prone to depression in the fourth quarter and often find it harder to maintain the diverse social network essential to a healthy brain.

Special issues for Singles: Introverted singles should be particularly wary of this fumble. Everyone needs some human touch or a companion. There is a reason people with four-legged friends tend to do better in the fourth quarter. A dog can even help with your exercise program.

Kaizen (small steps to success) ideas: Read an article from a different source (not the Internet!) than normal. Have an engaging conversation with your best friend where you take the opposite position from normal.

Potential Red Zone Fumble #16: Losing Faith

Many of those we interviewed for this book have lost faith in a higher power a few times in their lives. Some had never had faith to begin with. It's beyond the scope of this book to delve deeply into spiritual matters, but the evidence is clear – a spiritual "family" (church, synagogue, mosque or other religious body) has been shown to a) intervene when fumbles are imminent and b) help when someone fumbles in the fourth quarter and needs help getting back on track.

Having faith in something beyond this earth has helped many people deal better with horrible tragedies involving friends, family or community that could have created a cascading fumble effect in their own life.

Avoiding fumbles: Whatever your spiritual center, make every effort to stay engaged.

Recovering fumbles: If you've had a crisis of faith, spend time discussing the reasons with those you consider closest in your spiritual family. You may be surprised how many have had similar experiences.

Dangers: Loss of initiative. Fear of the unknown. Developing anxiety or depression.

Action plan: Take lost faith seriously. Try to find your spiritual center again. Look for likeminded people, even if it's at a place of worship that isn't your normal place to go.

Mars/Venus Considerations: Men seem to have more difficulties with lost faith than women, but both sexes are prone to uncertainty and faith crises at multiple times in their lives.

Special issues for Singles: Equal opportunities for fumbles.

Kaizen (small steps to success) ideas: make one visit to your favorite church, synagogue, mosque or spiritual renewal center. Talk to a leader in that organization.

More Help

Other potential mistakes related to **wellness** fumbles, available at www.FourthQuartersFumbles.com:

"Wellness" Worksheet

Personal assessment: Rate the following statements from 1 to 5:

1 = this statement doesn't describe me

5 = this statement is exactly like me

"I exercise regularly."

Rating: 1   2   3   4   5

Personal assessment: Rate the following statements from 1 to 5:

"I eat well most of the time."

Rating: 1   2   3   4   5

Personal assessment: Rate the following statements from 1 to 5:

"I sleep well most of the time."

Rating: 1   2   3   4   5

Personal assessment: Rate the following statements from 1 to 5:

"My spiritual life is strong."

Rating: 1   2   3   4   5

The one person in my life who has pursued wellness in the most balanced way is: _____

_____

My one Kaizen (small step to success) step will be: _____

_____

CHAPTER 8

Social Networks Rule Even in the Fourth Quarter

It's absurd to divide people into good and bad. People are either charming or tedious.

– Oscar Wilde

Some people we know have had to endure tedious people for so long in their careers that they avoid social events in the fourth quarter just to steer clear of boring conversations about which politician is making mistakes, who is sick, who died, and what aches, pains, and all manner of unfortunate aging issues are vexing the speaker.

Social networks are well known to be a key ingredient in happiness and life success prior to the fourth quarter. They don't have to include the party circuit; many happy people do great with small two-couple dinner gatherings and the occasional mixer. Good social networks are even more critical in the fourth quarter of life because other social activities (like raising children or working) are declining in time and importance.

Potential Red-Zone Fumble #17: Abandoning an Existing Social Network

I have seen people enter their fourth quarter of life and decide to leave their well-established friends and social network for a variety of reasons. Being closer to children and grandchildren is the number-one reason, followed by a desire to return to their home state or hometown. Finding adventure is also cited by some for leaving their existing networks or getting away from difficult family members.

Leaving an existing network is usually suggested by the spouse or life partner who has the least robust network. This leaves the remaining partner in a difficult position, especially if the more socially vibrant partner subsequently gets ill or dies.

Leaving an existing network to be closer to certain children and grandchildren can also backfire when that family moves for work-related reasons, which happens frequently these days.

Avoiding fumbles: Consider the *Why?* and the *How?* when deciding on the *Who?* and the *Where?* Have good, solid reasons for leaving an existing social network. Test out the new community you're considering by spending 2 to 4 weeks there renting a home near where you think you would like to live, in various seasons of the year.

Recovering fumbles: If you've moved for the wrong reasons, find ways to spend time back home. Moving back should be considered if you're convinced it's the best move; don't be concerned about what people think. It's your life and you have to make good decisions throughout the fourth quarter to have a better chance of fewer fumbles and more happiness.

Dangers: Disagreements with a life partner. Gray divorce. Developing anxiety or depression.

Action plan: Carefully weigh any decisions that involve moving away from existing friends or family.

Mars/Venus considerations: It has been our experience that men push for change more frequently in the fourth quarter but then have more difficulty adjusting to new friends and a new setting than women. Take your time and talk through the options with trusted friends and advisors.

Special issues for singles: Equal opportunities for fumbles.

Kaizen (small steps to success) ideas: Do a pro-and-con list. Talk to one person who moved away from his or her home base in the fourth quarter.

Potential Red-Zone Fumble #18: Not Tending the "Friends Garden"

Social networks are not fixed. How many good, true friends do you have? Two? Three? Are they the same friends you had 10 or 20 years ago? Staying connected and engaged with your friends may seem easy since you think you'll have more free time in the fourth quarter. Trips to see or spend adventure time with children and grandchildren will take you away from your friends. If you're comfortable and proficient with texting, e-mails, and other modern technology, staying in touch is easy. Staying truly engaged can be more difficult.

Friends and family have their own challenges during the fourth quarter. Are you ready to be patient when your close circle isn't immediately available when you need them? Ready to invest a lot of time listening without necessary feeling the need to offer suggestions? Ready to jump in and help a friend when other priorities are tugging at you?

Do you have a leaky network, losing friends or family to moving, illness, or death? Adding friends later in life can be helpful in making sure that you always have someone you like and respect that you can call and ask to breakfast, lunch, or an event as the fourth quarter progresses.

Avoiding fumbles: Be available and try to stay engaged with your existing network. Develop your social network even deeper later in life.

Recovering fumbles: Leaky networks can be fixed, but fixing the leaks works best when you stay engaged and interesting. Networks tend to not be as friendly to grumpy or anxious people.

One of our clients was a member of a Panera men's club that met every week for breakfast. He noticed his blood pressure and anxiety spiked around the same time, and friends and family noticed the same thing. Sitting around and talking about politics, how things are changing, and how the world was generally going down the drain is not a good recipe for mental health. He left the group, lost some acquaintances, but was able to then develop some great new friends. As a bonus, he is now off multiple medications for anxiety and high blood pressure.

Dangers: Disagreements with a life partner. Gray divorce. Developing anxiety or depression.

Action plan: Have a system where you check in regularly with friends and family. Find ways to add friends selectively along the way.

Mars/Venus considerations: Many women are able to nurture and build social networks better than men. This means men need to be more intentional and thoughtful about how they tend the garden. But as with any generality, it doesn't always hold true.

Special issues for singles: Occasionally more danger for introverted singles. New friends often get cultivated via the more outgoing partner in a relationship.

Kaizen (small steps to success) ideas: Engage one acquaintance or even a stranger in a conversation today.

Special stage-of-life issues:

Stage 1 (go-go): Good social networks are critical for most people in the fourth quarter.

Stage 2 (slow-go): Tending the social network in stage 2 can be one of the hardest things to do as friends and family become less available or disappear from your life.

Stage 3 (no-go): If you've tended the garden well, your social network should still be healthy in stage 3. If you've moved far away and haven't added new friends, it may be lonely at the end of life.

Potential Red-Zone Fumble #19:
Elder Abuse

Isolation is the foundation that all elder abuse is built on.

— Kerri Kasem (daughter of famed radio personality Casey Kasem)

Elder abuse takes many forms and is inflicted by someone close to the victim in over 70% of cases according to AARP. Casey Kasem, the famous radio personality who died at age 82 in 2014, was a victim of elder abuse. Remember when CNN ran the headline: "Casey Kasem is missing?" His story is a cautionary one that includes a late-life remarriage to a younger woman who isolated him from his family and made his later life miserable, likely also reducing his lifetime. I was recently with one of his daughters, Kerri, who is working with states around the country to make anti-elder abuse laws more stringent.

Other examples include the child who has financial or drug-related problems and keeps "borrowing" from mom or dad. If they have power of attorney, often the gifts become theft, and law enforcement has to be involved.

Fake or irresponsible contractors are well known for abusing seniors. "I noticed your roof needs fixing. My crew is around the corner. I can give you a good deal." Then they do incomplete or shoddy work, or they take the down payment and disappear.

Avoiding fumbles: Surround yourself with trustworthy people who help with decision-making as you get older. Have advocates (which can include your financial planner, accountant, and attorney) who know the signs of elder abuse. People aging in place at home in their slow-go or no-go years are more likely to be victims of elder abuse.

Recovering fumbles: In some cases, early intervention can prevent elder abuse. In others, getting adult protective services in your area involved may be needed.

Dangers: Financial theft. Health problems. Family stress. Developing anxiety or depression.

Action plan: Avoid isolation. If a person is trying to isolate you for any reason, let someone you trust know.

As discussed throughout this book, be careful not to go overboard avoiding this fumble! If you're single and not in a serious relationship, and if you meet someone nice in stage 1, 2, or 3 of the fourth quarter, be open to the possibilities. We have seen many more people blossom in the fourth quarter as a result of a new relationship than ones that end in misery or elder abuse.

Mars/Venus considerations: Both sexes are victims of elder abuse in many different forms.

Special issues for singles: More danger because of more daily isolation. Consider retirement-community options.

Kaizen (small steps to success) ideas: Trust but verify in all new relationships. Ask your life partner or closest friend how they plan to avoid isolation later in life.

More Help

To learn more about **social network** fumbles, go to: www.FourthQuartersFumbles.com.

"Social Network" Worksheet

Personal assessment: Rate the following statements from 1 to 5:

> 1 = this statement doesn't describe me
>
> 5 = this statement is exactly like me

"I have a strong social network."

Rating: 1   2   3   4   5

Personal assessment: Rate the following statements from 1 to 5:

"I'm isolated and lonely."

Rating: 1   2   3   4   5

Personal assessment: Rate the following statements from 1 to 5:

"My circle of friends are exactly who I want to be around."

Rating: 1   2   3   4   5

The one person in my life who has a good social network is: _____

_____

My one Kaizen (small step to success) step will be: _____

_____

CHAPTER 9

Communicate Until the Cows Come Home

Speak clearly, if you speak at all; carve every word before you let it fall.

– Oliver Wendell Holmes

Communication breakdowns are common throughout life but are especially so in the fourth quarter. *How* you communicate is every bit as important as *what* you're trying to say. Many family and friends "assume" someone else knows what they are feeling or thinking. The potential for miscommunication is even greater as brain chemistry changes or patience wears thin as you age.

The excellent book *How to Say It to Seniors: Closing the Communication Gap with Our Elders* by David Solie suggests the following process when communication blows up, senior to senior or senior to child:

> ***Back off and reexamine.*** We need to review our efforts to communicate as objectively as possible. Did we present an idea in a rushed way? At the wrong time? Did we withhold key information that we thought was relevant?
>
> ***Return to a more neutral position.*** Most people don't appreciate anyone coming back to a sore topic time and time again. People in the fourth quarter find it especially annoying. Let a tough topic sit and wait for a better time to revisit it, or find a different way to approach the topic, such as sending an article that explains what you were trying to say.
>
> ***Don't take a negative reaction personally.*** Did you take your children's reactions at face value when they were young? Maybe the timing was off. Moods change during the day; sometimes trying the discussion in a different way at a different time of day can work better.
>
> ***Words matter.*** Did you use provocative words when you pitched an idea? Did you express it as, "Of course you'll agree with me when I say . . ." versus "I wonder what you think about . . . ?"

Prepare in advance. Luck favors the prepared. I've often found that rehearsing a difficult message with a friend or loved one can prepare me better for reactions I may get.

Let's dig deeper into the all-important **emotional-intelligence (EQ) factors** that often spell the difference between an average and a great fourth quarter of life.

Here are five key EQ factors:

Self-awareness. The ability to recognize an emotion as it "happens" is the key to your EQ. Developing self-awareness requires tuning in to your true feelings. If you evaluate your emotions, you can manage them. The major elements of self-awareness are:

- *Emotional awareness:* your ability to recognize your own emotions and their effects.
- *Self-confidence:* sureness about your self-worth and capabilities. Confidence is one area we see erode in the fourth quarter for many individuals.

Self-regulation. You often have little control over when you experience emotions. You can, however, have some say in how long an emotion will last by using a number of techniques to alleviate negative emotions such as anger, anxiety, or depression, which are all sources of fourth quarter fumbles. These techniques include recasting a situation in a more positive light, taking a long walk, meditation and choosing who you associate with in the fourth quarter.

As mentioned earlier, we have a client who found he was having heart and blood-pressure issues every Thursday morning and Sunday afternoon. The culprits were his Panera Bread men's group, which met on Thursday mornings and sat around and talked about how bad the world was, and the Sunday news shows, which he always watched, with their similar "talk about everything bad" focus. He changed his men's group and cut out Sunday news shows. He is now feeling great and off all his medications!

Self-regulation involves:

- *Self-control:* managing disruptive impulses.
- *Trustworthiness:* maintaining standards of honesty and integrity.
- *Conscientiousness:* taking responsibility for your own actions.
- *Adaptability* (also known as *resiliency*): handling change with flexibility, a key fourth quarter challenge.
- *Innovation:* being open to new ideas, which can be harder to do as you age.

Motivation. To motivate yourself to keep going even when you're entering the slow-go stage, you need clear goals and a positive attitude. Although you may have a predisposition to either a positive or a negative attitude, you can with effort and practice learn to think more positively. If you catch negative thoughts as they occur, you can reframe them in more positive terms, which will help you achieve your fourth quarter goals.

A classic resource here is Martin Seligman's book, *Learned Optimism: How to Change Your Mind and Your Life*. In my travels I've run into many very successful people who said this book helped them break through barriers and maintain a high and sustained level of success well into the fourth quarter.

Motivation is made up of:

- *Lifelong learning*: seeking both formal and informal opportunities to expand your knowledge. Some think when they retire learning isn't important anymore. It is actually more important if you intend to stay sharp and away from destructive influences. A constant striving to improve or to meet a standard of excellence can be just as important in the fourth quarter as long as it doesn't constantly annoy your life partner or friends.

- *Commitment*: aligning with the goals of your family and friends.

- *Initiative*: readying yourself to act on opportunities. Staying young at heart often involves spontaneity, which can wane as you age if you're not focused on occasionally doing something fun that is unplanned.

- *Optimism*: pursuing goals persistently despite obstacles and setbacks.

From Norman Vincent Peale's classic book, *The Power of Positive Thinking* to *The Rational Optimist* by Matt Ridley, the fourth quarter is a great time to sharpen your ability to see the good in the world.

Empathy. The ability to recognize how people feel is important to success in your life and becomes even more critical in the fourth quarter. The more skillful you are at discerning the feelings of others, the better you can control the signals you send them. An empathetic person excels at:

- *Developing others*: sensing what others need to progress and bolstering their abilities. Some of our most successful healthy-aging clients have several mentoring and people projects going at the same time, including coming up with creative ideas for helping their grandchildren thrive.

- Leveraging diversity: cultivating opportunities through diverse people. Seniors often hang around the same people all the time, not a good formula for lifelong learning and avoiding boredom.

- Understanding others: discerning the feelings behind the needs and wants of others.

Social skills. The development of good interpersonal skills is critical to success in life. If you weren't a people person in the first three quarters of your life, can you change in the fourth quarter? The answer is yes! We've seen many amazing transformations where even died-in-the-wool introverts learned to engage with family and friends better in the fourth quarter.

One prominent introverted man we work with blossomed after his extravert wife passed away. He had been content to be a listener for many decades, but after his wife (who he had dubbed "the great communicator") died, he decided he had better improve his communication or he would become lonely and wither away.

Among the most useful social skills are:

- *Influence*: being persuasive without being overbearing.
- *Communication*: sending clear messages.

- *Being a change catalyst*: initiating or managing change (especially if your spouse or life partner isn't inclined to make the changes that are needed).

- *Conflict management*: understanding, negotiating, and resolving disagreements. The old saying, "I married you for life, not for lunch" plays out in the fourth quarter with more potential conflict points. If you grew up in a co-dependent household, and those tendencies have stayed around, what better time than the fourth quarter to unpack those issues with a professional and learn healthy conflict resolution?

- *Building bonds*: nurturing family and friend relationships is still important!

- *Collaboration and cooperation*: working with others toward shared goals.

Potential Red-Zone Fumble #20: Poor Communication with Your Life Partner

It is said that absence makes the heart grow fonder. However, being with someone for longer periods of time in the fourth quarter is a good way to grow less fond. Remember the axiom: "I married you for better or worse, not for lunch"? As people live longer, finding interesting things to discuss can become more challenging. Longer periods of silence can be fine unless one partner views silence as not caring anymore.

Not caring or demonstrating you care is a major reason for the rise of gray divorce; closely behind this is the problem of more angry, contentious, and anxious communications between life partners.

> **Avoiding fumbles:** Living a balanced life can help. How does your fourth quarter wheel look (see Appendix 6)? If it looks like a flat tire on one side or worse, all around, you may be in danger of being neither interested in or interesting to your partner in the fourth quarter.

Recovering fumbles: Marriage counseling is rare in the fourth quarter, mostly because of the belief that if we made it this far, we should be able to get to the finish line. Or one partner thinks this is admitting something is broken. Clients who go through therapy describe the main benefit as "getting back to more positive communication."

Here are the three reasons most often cited, in addition to better communication, for marital counseling: (1) when one or both partners consider having an affair, or one has had an affair; (2) when the partners can't reconcile differences, including key fourth quarter decisions; and (3) when the couple just seems to be roommates (we've heard some say, "It's too expensive to get divorced, and it isn't that bad living together"; these situations seldom turn out well for one or both partners).

Dangers: Disagreements with a life partner. Gray divorce. Developing anxiety or depression.

Action plan: Seek to be both interested in what happens to your life partner and interesting by staying well-read and up to date on current events that are interesting to your life partner. **Go beyond the Golden Rule to the Platinum rule: Do unto others as *they* would like to be treated.** Avoid the attitude of: "My opinion is the only one that counts."

Mars/Venus considerations: Guys, *interested* doesn't mean trying to fix whatever is wrong in your partner's life without getting tacit permission first. Didn't you learn this from the numerous other times this didn't work earlier in this or other relationships?

Interesting doesn't mean taking sports, politics, or your favorite hobby discussions to another deeper level. Remember when you were dating and it was more important to know what was on your date's mind rather than droning on about your own brilliance?

Men and women who try to have a regular date night (again in moderation, not every night in the fourth quarter!) and do something special together have better long-term communication and fourth quarter results.

Special issues for singles: Not applicable, although crunchy communication is a great early warning sign if you're dating someone who could become a life partner.

Kaizen (small steps to success) ideas: Do one thing today for your life partner just because it used to make him or her giddy.

Potential Red-Zone Fumble #21: Communicating With Your Family

Families have history. Not all of that history is peaches and cream. Historical rifts trip up peace accords between nation-states almost as often as they do in families. Do you find it more difficult to communicate with your children these days? Does it seem as if they have a different approach to raising their children or don't agree with your worldview?

One of our clients almost disconnected from Facebook because of political commentary he disagreed with going back and forth between his children and his children's friends. He and his daughter had a tough series of communications before he decided to pivot back to the more important family issues that would still be present after the current political scene has changed. Are you going to cut off great stories and pictures of the grandchildren as a result of political winds that are likely to change in 4 years or less?

Should you keep your financial, long-term-care, and estate-planning cards close to your vest as you age, only letting your children know bits and pieces of your fourth quarter plan, or should you move towards full disclosure? I think it depends on the children, how grounded they are, and how much you have them involved in your estate plan. Have a grown child in his or her late fifties who has your back-up power of attorney? It's a pretty good idea to read that person in on your entire estate plan, including long-term-care preferences. If you don't trust your child will carry out your wishes, find another person for this important duty. Consider not just *what* you're going to share but also *how* it will be communicated.

> **Avoiding fumbles:** Begin letting your children know what your fourth quarter plans are early on. If you have responsible and not-so-responsible children, it's still fine to have a family meeting and share the broad outlines of your plan. Choose a time when thoughtful listening and discussion is easy. Having grandchildren in the room or other distractions (like the big sports game) is rarely a good venue for important conversations.

> **Recovering fumbles:** There is never a better time than now to begin improved communication. Want to extend an olive branch to a child that you don't communicate well with? Cut out or print an article on some fourth quarter topic you find interesting and send it to that child with a handwritten note: "Thinking about these issues. Would love your input when you have a chance."

Have a deep rift with a child? There are dozens of good ways to get them back into your life. Perhaps your life partner, another child, or one of your siblings is still in touch with the estranged child; that person can communicate that you'd like to have a conversation. Note that "burying the hatchet" and rehashing old arguments is rarely a good idea. Read *When Sorry Isn't Enough: Making Things Right with Those You Love* by Gary Chapman and

Jennifer Thomas or watch Jen Thomas's TEDx talk, "Getting the Last Word with Apology."

Dangers: Family disagreements. Not having your wishes followed when you're incapacitated or die.

Action plan: Find ways to begin conversations. Keep it simple. Your financial advisor or planner can help facilitate these discussions if that's part of his or her service offering. Communicate more over time, especially as your own ability to manage your affairs becomes more tenuous.

Mars/Venus considerations: Men are generally more prone to cutting off communication with certain children who haven't marched to their view of a successful life.

Special issues for singles: Equal opportunity for fumbles.

Kaizen (small steps to success) ideas: Make a small gesture to communicate with one of your family members.

More Help

To learn more about **communication** fumbles, go to: www.FourthQuartersFumbles.com.

- **Hostile Takeover of the Household** – one of our OCD (obsessive compulsive disorder) clients retired and proceeded to reorganize the kitchen – twice. It created significant issues with his wife, who was the main cook in the family.

- **Comments that Shut Down Communication** – being right, and making sure your life partner and others know it, isn't always the best plan in the fourth quarter.

"Communication" Worksheet

Personal assessment: Rate the following statements from 1 to 5:

1 = this statement doesn't describe me

5 = this statement is exactly like me

"I have good communication skills."

Rating: 1   2   3   4   5

Personal assessment: Rate the following statements from 1 to 5:

"I listen to learn rather than listen to respond."

Rating: 1   2   3   4   5

Personal assessment: Rate the following statements from 1 to 5:

"My relationship with my life partner and family is strong."

Rating: 1   2   3   4   5

Who do you know who has good communication, especially listening, skills? _____

_____

My one Kaizen (small step to success) step to better communication will be: _____

_____

CHAPTER 10

Thoughtful Estate Planning

Life should begin with age and its privileges and accumulations, and end with youth and its capacity to splendidly enjoy such advantages.

– Mark Twain

Most people spend very little time on estate planning. Contemplating not being in command of your faculties or your life, followed by one's death, and thinking through all the scenarios isn't in the top 10 (or even top 100) list for most people. Thoughtful estate planning, where you consider not just the tax and inheritance laws but also your unique family and heirs, can lead to fewer fumbles before and after your death, saving time, money, and many hard feelings.

Potential Red-Zone Fumble #22:
Who Will Make Important Health-Care Decisions for You If You Can't?

Health-care decisions are often made by a life partner or spouse when a person can't communicate his or her own wishes. Have you discussed how you would like those decisions made?

If you're single, does your health-care attorney-in-fact have similar ideas to your own on health care, including how much intervention may be appropriate in more life-threatening situations? One of our single clients decided that his only brother was the logical choice but was concerned they disagreed on most later-in-life intervention possibilities. He decided to name his minister, his brother, and his long-time trusted advisor as co-attorneys-in-fact.

> **Cautionary tale:** At a major West Coast conference in San Francisco a few years ago, a behavioral-finance expert presented a study that showed even when we hear and see identical information we can reach startlingly different conclusions. In the study, 600 surgeons were provided the same facts about a cancer diagnosis and potential prescriptive actions, radiation, or surgery; 300 of them were given the patient facts in a positive way (90% of the patients will survive radiation treatment), and the other 300 were given the facts in a negative way (10% of the patients will die with radiation treatments). The 300 surgeons given the positive facts had a radically different mix of

recommendations than the surgeons given the same information in a negative fashion.

Another study cited by the Center for Medical Consumers showed that a high proportion of the doctors who do delicate medical procedures have relatively little experience with the procedures! And numerous other studies show that patients have a much higher risk of serious injury or death at the hands of a surgeon or hospital that infrequently handles that procedure.

Medicine is both an art and a science; make sure both you and your health-care advocate (ideally listening to the options for you in the room, not second hand, when you're faced with a major medical decision) are good listeners. Ask lots of questions. Don't be afraid to get second and even third opinions, especially when critical decisions are involved. And make sure your health-care attorney-in-fact knows how to be a good health-care advocate.

Avoiding fumbles: Choose a health-care attorney-in-fact and successor who can be available for key decisions and have good common sense. Note this individual is often a life partner/ spouse, but the successor is sometimes a different person than the Durable Power of Attorney choice. Making health-care decisions is very different emotionally than financial decisions.

Advancing health-care technology may require different decisions in the future as once-fatal diseases become treatable.

Recovering fumbles: Poor health-care choices often lead down a path of no return. However, an estimated 40% of cognitive declines are treatable and reversible. If you discover your health-care attorney-in-fact hasn't made good decisions, have a discussion with that person. Then decide whether you need to make a new choice.

Dangers: Health-care choices that don't reflect your wishes. Life-threatening results. Disagreements with a life partner.

Action plan: Choose your health-care attorney-in-fact and successor carefully. Communicate about your wishes and preferences. Don't assume someone knows what you want.

Mars/Venus considerations: Equal fumble potential.

Special issues for singles: Critical to have someone you trust to make good decisions on your behalf.

Kaizen (small steps to success) ideas: Ask yourself today, perhaps with your favorite adult beverage, "Who has the right frame of mind to make health care decisions on my behalf?"

Other fumble avoidance resources: *You Bet Your Life: The 10 Mistakes Every Patient Makes* by Trisha Torrey.

Potential Red-Zone Fumble #23: Too Much Focus on Tax Avoidance

I've been involved in very sophisticated estate planning for high net-worth individuals and families for over three decades. For much of that time, future estate taxes have been a major potential liability for these clients. Most don't like the concept of having assets that have already been taxed in one or more ways being taxed yet again when assets pass to their heirs.

Fumbles occur in this area when someone is overly obsessed with avoiding sending Uncle Sam "one thin dime" they don't have to. This goal usually meant implementing multiple advanced estate techniques linked together, creating a complex array of documents that can be hard to understand, burdensome to maintain over many decades, and hard to communicate to future generations.

More disturbing is the number of times I've seen someone focus so much on tax avoidance that they almost missed some basic planning for themselves and the next generation. In one case, my client and I spent over an hour with an estate attorney discussing ways the client could minimize estate tax at death. The client had said this was his number-one goal and the attorney prioritized the meeting discussion around this area. As the attorney was apologizing for needing to wrap up and get to his next meeting, we mentioned the fact the client had a child with spending problems, out-of-date trustees, and powers of attorney. The fumble potential in these mistakes was enormous. Thankfully the client didn't die before the next meeting; we refocused on the nontax basics and buttoned up the overall estate plan.

Today's laws allow much more to be passed to the next generation without estate tax. Many families can now follow the KISS (Keep It Sweet and Simple) principle with less-complex documents. However, there exists a danger that too simple may inadvertently create a fumble in another area or that estate laws become more onerous as new politicians get in power in the future.

Avoiding fumbles: Balance minimizing taxes with making sure other fumbles discussed in this chapter are also avoided.

Recovering fumbles: If you already have many complex documents, some are likely irrevocable, meaning they can't be changed. Unless they can be changed! There are many estate attorneys we work with who have become experts at decanting, or removing assets from irrevocable trusts.

Dangers: Focusing on avoiding taxes when other potential estate fumbles need discussion. Complex estate-distribution plans. High cost to maintain over many decades. Confusion over who gets what when.

Action plan: Review your estate plan in light of current taxes and possible future tax scenarios. Focus as much time on non-tax estate-review issues as the tax-avoidance area.

Mars/Venus considerations: Men tend to get more focused on tax-avoidance techniques, to the exclusion of softer estate issues (such as who should get grandmother's heirloom diamond ring) than women.

Special issues for singles: Same potential for fumbles.

Kaizen (small steps to success) ideas: For one estate-update review, focus entirely on nontax issues to make sure you've covered potential fumble areas.

More Help

Other potential mistakes related to **estate-planning** fumbles, available at www.FourthQuartersFumbles.com:

- **Balancing Estate Taxes with Income Taxes** – often income taxes after death are a bigger issue than estate taxes.

- **Beneficiary Designations** – outdated beneficiaries can create lots of headaches after your death.

- **Giving Money to Children Who Can't Handle It** – a classic issue – you don't want your hard earned wealth squandered after your death.

- **Poor Charitable Planning** – many don't consider all the options to provide financial or leadership resources to a favorite community group or non-profit organization.

- **Poor Sentimental Asset Planning** – do your children really want your china? How to avoid family fights after your death.

- **Choosing the Wrong Trustees** – trusts can be a good way to protect money for future generations, but only if it's managed properly and the right directions have been put in for the trustee.

- **Dying Without a Will** – the intestate rules will likely pass money to places that wouldn't be your first choice, plus increase costs and delay the estate distribution.

- **Who Will Pay Your Bills if You're Temporarily or Permanently Disabled?** – make sure the primary and secondary attorney-in-fact are up to this task.

- **Losing Your Will** – can a trusted person find your original signed will after your death?

- **Hoarding** – making fear-based gifting decisions, a behavioral finance fumble that often occurs in the fourth quarter "slow-go" and "no-go" years.

- **Avoiding Probate at a High Cost –** many people are so fearful of probate, which with some estate profiles and in some states isn't a huge issue, that they will turn their estate plan into a giant pretzel, which can then create unnecessary fumbles.

"Estate Planning" Worksheet

Personal assessment: Rate the following statements from 1 to 5:

1 = this statement doesn't describe me

5 = this statement is exactly like me

"I have a well thought out estate plan."

Rating: 1   2   3   4   5

Personal assessment: Rate the following statements from 1 to 5:

"I strongly believe my health care wishes will be carried out well by the people I've designated in my health care power of attorney document."

Rating: 1   2   3   4   5

Personal assessment: Rate the following statements from 1 to 5:

"I don't really understand my estate plan."

Rating: 1   2   3   4   5

How would you describe your understanding of how all facets of your estate plan will work in your *no-go* years and after your death? _____

_____

The one person you trust the most to make good health care decisions is: _____

_____

My one Kaizen (small step to success) step to strengthen my estate plan will be: _____

_____

CHAPTER 11

Getting Your Living Options Right

You're better off being 5 years too early choosing a retirement community to move to, instead of 5 minutes too late when a health event may mean the retirement community you like declines to let you live there.

— A Life Care Industry maxim

Let's begin this discussion by considering the positives around staying in your own home, or a downsized version, late into the fourth quarter or even to the end of your fourth quarter.

- It's familiar, and you have positive memories and experiences.

- It's easier than moving and thinking about what to do with all your "stuff" that the children or grandchildren now don't want.

- You can keep your dog and cat, or have as many of them as you want, without anyone saying anything to you. Animals who are good friends have been shown to be a positive factor in healthy aging.

- You can work in your own garden. Scientists have discovered a bacterium in soil that has a calming effect, sort of nature's version of Prozac. Being outdoors with flowers and sunshine is a powerful happiness factor for many people

- You have room for the children or grandchildren to come and visit.

Now for a few of the potential negatives related to moving away from your own home to a retirement or life-care community:

- A big issue is often the loss of independence and a recognition this may be your last move.

- It's a new environment; if you're more introverted, this change will not feel like a good thing unless you already have friends in a particular retirement community who will help you get acclimated.

- It goes against scripts you learned as a child that having your own home is the American dream. You're giving up on that dream. More accurately, you're reprioritizing that dream to other areas of your life.

Staying in your home isn't a panacea. Getting things fixed around the home becomes more of a hassle factor as you get deeper into the fourth quarter. Your *who* may suffer: you run more of a risk of becoming isolated as your friends and family move or die.

What usually triggers a move to a more aging-friendly home?

- The elder(s) or their family feel there are safety issues in the current home.

- A negative health event occurs.

- Transportation to places the elder(s) like and need to go becomes an issue.

- The elder(s) can't keep up the existing home.

- The elder(s) or the family see a deteriorating amount of interaction with others.

- Elders simply like to plan ahead (unfortunately only a small percentage move for this reason).

Some people view moving out of the family home as natural and even an exciting step to begin a new chapter of life. Others view it as the next step towards death, especially since that was the view of many of our parents back in the days when aging in place was the only option unless you wanted to end up in a not-so-nice nursing home.

In the "old days," most people assumed they would stay in their homes until they died or were forced into a nursing home. Most nursing homes were less-than-pleasant places where friends and family would dread to visit. The late stages of the fourth quarter were assumed to be dismal; anything was preferable to ending up in a nursing home.

Today, the options for continuing-care retirement communities, or the newer term, *life-care communities*, are much better. Options are so good, we've had many clients who have trouble picking the one they like best. However, the majority of people we work with still want to stay in their home for as long as possible, some forever.

I visited a client a few years ago recovering from a fall in a "new and improved" nursing home that I had visited 20 years before. The prior experience was a negative assault on the senses, especially sights and smells and the feel that this was "God's waiting room." My later visit was completely different. I was told by a very pleasant and well-trained person at the front desk that I should take a left at the pottery class and then a right by the coffee bar. My client was actually smiling when I arrived and felt like his rehabilitation was going "better than expected."

New options to consider

There are a variety of new options for fourth quarter living. They include:

- "Cluster" communities where people over age 55 have clustered around service providers that are senior friendly. Without the right family member or a good geriatric care manager nearby, fumbles can happen in these communities when transitioning deeper into the fourth quarter.

- Cruise ships are becoming more popular since many of them now offer services similar to a Life Care community.

With the massive surge of Baby Boomers moving into the fourth quarter of life, it's likely there will be many new living options available, including new downsizing options built.

Here is another example that demonstrates the *how* can be just as important, if not more so, than the *what* of your fourth quarter decisions and actions. Ken from Dallas had lost his wife of many years. His children were concerned that he would become a hermit in the family home, a fear that he shared. They convinced him to buy into a robust Presbyterian retirement community close to where they lived. Ken was considering a patio home there, and again the children encouraged him to stay in the mainstream of people and life. He bought an apartment in a newer section under construction.

Today, he is certain this path has been the best for him, even though the transition has been challenging at times. Ken stays connected to outside golfing friends, although some have died or can't play anymore. He has made new friends at the retirement community, performing one of the best jobs of "tending the friends garden" I've seen.

Ken is a prolific writer and is even studying better writing at the tender age of 82. Below is an excerpt from one of his musings right after he moved into the retirement community. It captures the struggle to adjust to so many transitions all at once, while enjoying the peace that has come from being in a place where other fumbles won't interfere with his goal to make the best of this "lemonish part of life."

Independent Living

A cold winter day, just after a sleepless night and dawn, sitting on my miniature balcony, wrapped in a fleece blanket, drinking steaming coffee that has become such an integral part of life, almost as important as the daily required walks with my Shih Tzu, Sophie. I look out at a large pond dyed lagoon blue and enjoy the 12 new Mallards that have joined the pair, who have previously taken permanent possession of the pond. I wonder are these new ducks visiting, or will they, like me, become permanent residents in this secure, sedentary, peaceful environment, this Eden for the old? The center of the pond boasts a fountain that bursts 20 feet into the air and makes a quarter rainbow to the West as it is revealed by the Sunrise. Conflict arises in me again as I weigh the beauty of the fountain against its angry sound. Fountains, coffee, ponds, and Mallards have replaced most of the active parts of my previous life with all its dynamic concerns.

This new beautiful building hosts 48 apartments. A full slate of potential new friends and activities are listed on my refrigerator door, most of which I feel too young or too old to attend.

No more wife, no more job, no house, no yard to mow, no pickup, hunting, fishing, sailing, travel, skiing, cruising, gardening, church leadership, and far fewer friends for whom I can share deepest cares. I sip coffee and cherish the thought of still having my three children and families living near. . . . A mixed bag of good often immersed in the awareness of life gone for good and the challenge to make lemonade from this lemonish part of life.

For those who are determined to age in place in their homes, or a downsized less-maintenance-intensive version, until they die, the future holds many technological advances that will make life less fumble-prone. However, the risk of becoming a hermit is still high, leading to several dozen of the fumbles discussed in this book. Projects like the one below may someday lessen the risk of some of these fumbles later in life.

One of my clients is working on a robotics project to create a version of "Rosy the robot" from the old Jetsons cartoon TV show. The vision is that Rosy will be a futuristic caregiver, with the ability to cook over 180 different meals, discuss your favorite interests like an old friend, and help with cleaning and other life-care needs. Eventually Rosy will also be able to provide caregiving under the definition of daily living activities: bathing, dressing, transferring (moving to and from a bed or a chair), toileting, eating, caring for incontinence. Most long-term-care insurance policies begin benefits if you can't do two of these six or have severe memory impairment.

At first, I doubted that many people I know would embrace this futuristic Rosy. Early versions may be clunky, and most of us want a more human touch as we're aging. Then I was presented with the ultimate vision of this project in ten plus years and realized the future, yet again, may provide wonders we can't even imagine.

And the real miracles lie in what medical science is developing for our bodies that go well beyond just technology to make our lives easier or less fumble-prone around the house.

Potential Red-Zone Fumble #24: Not adjusting to Late-Stage Issues

We have many clients who have decided they want to age in place (stay at home) forever. We've already discussed some of the potential pitfalls of staying at home. Key fumbles we've seen are:

- Becoming a recluse, especially after the death of a life partner
- Not replacing inner circle friends when they die, become infirmed, or move away
- Poor nutrition late in the slow-go and into the no-go stage
- Depression leading to a variety of other ailments
- Failure to make the home aging-friendly
- Financial insecurity, because it is often more expensive to have caregiving done at home

This fumble could be because you're not truly prepared for what it means to stay in your own home, or a downsized version, late into the fourth quarter. It could also be a fumble because someone waited too long and couldn't transition well into the next phase of living in a continuing-care retirement community or other retirement community.

Avoiding fumbles: Be even more proactive in your quest to make the fourth quarter rewarding if you decide to stay in your home. Hire a specialist and make your home senior-friendly. Don't scrimp on this one! Are stairs as bad as they seem (fall danger) if they help keep your joints more nimble?

Make sure you always have at least five good friends or close family members nearby that you regularly interact with. Why five? People are busy in their lives and you need a robust network if you don't have the natural retirement-community network around you. Lose one of the five people? Replace that person! This is like the moat around the castle; if you're the king or queen of your domain, don't fall victim to a leaky moat.

Recovering fumbles: It's never too late to get more engaged with the world. It might not even be too late to reconsider moving to a retirement community. It becomes harder for some to adjust to retirement-community life and be accepted into the flow of the community late in the game, so more effort may be needed. Your team of professional advisors should be able to help you consider options and even make introductions.

Dangers: Deteriorating health. Isolation. Premature falls. Developing anxiety or depression. Failure of the fourth quarter plan because of excessive costs.

Action plan: If you're determined to stay in your own home, make sure you avoid becoming isolated. Consider using technology that will help your closest friends and family know if you aren't following your normal routine, such as opening the refrigerator door at least once per day.

Mars/Venus considerations: Men fall victim to this fumble more often than women.

Special issues for singles: More danger for singles, especially those without a good social network nearby. This is why many singles choose a retirement community over aging in place.

Kaizen (small steps to success) ideas: Google "aging in place" and read some of the articles.

Potential Red-Zone Fumble #25: Waiting Too Long

It's easy to procrastinate about a decision to leave your home or to go into a retirement community. Many people wait too long, have a health event, and the retirement community they want to be at won't let them in. The good news is many retirement communities will still let you in if one spouse has a health issue. But the one that will allow you in after the major health event may not be the one you really want to live in.

Another problem is that more people are waiting until they are almost in their no-go stage to enter a retirement community, and then they are not inclined to make friends or integrate into the community. Unhappiness and a variety of fumbles usually follow.

Avoiding fumbles: Make a decision and move towards your desired retirement-community home with intentionality.

Recovering fumbles: Widen your search area if your preferred retirement community won't accept you. If you're having trouble assimilating into the retirement-community culture, make extra efforts to meet people and engage in activities.

Dangers: Being forced to age in place at home. Cost or quality-of-care issues. Not enjoying the retirement-community experience. Conflict with life partner and family.

Action plan: Do your homework on various retirement or life care community options, get comfortable with the decision, and then move forward.

Mars/Venus considerations: Men tend to wait too long to move towards a retirement-community decision, although we've also seen a fair share of women procrastinate who don't want to leave the safe environment of their homes.

Special issues for singles: Equal fumble potential.

Kaizen (small steps to success) ideas: Take a tour of the retirement community most talked about in positive terms by your friends.

More Help

Other potential mistakes related to **living option** fumbles, available at www.FourthQuartersFumbles.com:

- **Downsizing to the Wrong Neighborhood** – you pick the right home, but not the right neighborhood. Friends don't visit as much and things you like to do are not as convenient.

- **Not Picking the Right Life-Care Community** – shopping for the right retirement community should be done with the same fervor as mapping out a dream vacation.

- **Split Households** – what if one life partner decides to stay in the family home and the other needs a life care community?

- **Assuming the Retirement Community You Like is Not Affordable** – turns out many "expensive" life care communities don't cost that much more than you're spending now when you consider the hidden living expense costs you save every week, including home upkeep.

"Living Options" Worksheet

Personal assessment: Rate the following statements from 1 to 5:
1 = this statement doesn't describe me
5 = this statement is exactly like me

"I have thought through the issues of
where I'll live as I transition through the fourth quarter."
Rating: 1   2   3   4   5

Who do you know who has a good future living options plan? ____

_____

My one Kaizen (small step to success) step to thoughtfully considering future living options will be: _____

_____

CONCLUSION

Avoid the Fumbles, Win the Game of Life!

It's virtually impossible to avoid some fumbles in the fourth quarter. Even my most forward-looking, mindful clients have had unexpected challenges that changed their primary game plan on multiple occasions.

Here is a summary of a few of the key actions to minimizing fumbles and, if you do experience a fumble, to support recovering to make your fourth quarter as much fun and as rewarding as the other quarters of your life. Like Benjamin Franklin, you can have a time when you can utilize your lifetime of skills and experience in a fourth quarter that future generations of your family will hold up as a role model.

This is not a one size fits all, because the fourth quarter is a time when one size fits one: you!

Know how fumbles happen and what others have done to avoid them or recover from them.

Health is your number-one asset in life. Focus more on the pursuit of wellness in the fourth quarter, not just absence of illness. Stay mobile as long as possible. Do lots of things to limber up your mind and body.

Explore and expand your *Why*, your reason to get out of bed every morning.

Nurture your *Who*. Don't face the challenges of the fourth quarter alone; you need a team of friends, family, and advisors to help you at different points in time to avoid or recover from fumbles. Perhaps even more important, this team should include the right people for the specific time and problem. Even one wrong perspective at any given time can put you in serious jeopardy.

How you do things matters in the fourth quarter! Consciously work on better decision-making. Have several friends or family members or advisors help you make better decisions.

Sharpen your bounce-back skills. Resiliency is a top predictor of fourth quarter success and it *can* be improved.

After you've done well on the above items, think long and hard about your *Where*. Be mindful that your *Where* can trip you up with many of the issues listed above.

Now make the fourth quarter the best it can be for you and your loved ones!

APPENDIX 1:

Fumble Likelihood Assessment

The following Fumble Likelihood Assessment will help determine your Fumbleocity™ score, you're likelihood to fumble in the fourth quarter. It combines the experiences of hundreds of people at different stages of the fourth quarter of their lives, providing advice on what they wish they had thought more about when they were entering the last quarter of their lives.

If you're approaching the fourth quarter, take the survey in that spirit and adjust your answers as if you're already wrestling with your *How Much?* (financial resources to accomplish your fourth quarter goals), *Why?* (why you should get out of bed in the morning), *Who?* (who you should associate with), and *Where?* (where you will live). Tying all these areas together is your *How?*, how do you do something that creates a lasting benefit.

If you're already in the go-go, slow-go or no-go stages of the fourth quarter, likewise adjust your answers. This is intended as a directional guide to highlight areas of potential fumbles and how to lessen the likelihood of fumbles and achieve fourth quarter happiness.

If one area stands out as a potential problem, focus on that part of this book. If you and your life partner both take the assessment, it will provide rich opportunities for good communication as you consider how to navigate the fourth quarter together and make joint decisions. Or it will create good opportunities for identifying friction points that need future work. If you're both fuming after this discussion, I suggest reading chapter 9, Communicate Until the Cows Come Home, let some time pass, and then try having the discussion again.

Go with the first, instinctive answer that comes to mind. Read the summary of that answer. Only if you really feel another answer absolutely, positively fits you should you change the answer. Total the point count for each of your answers at the end for the overall score.

Making Better Decisions

1.) How have you done in the past with major decisions?

A.) *Not very well.* (0 points)

Sorry to hear that. No time like the present to up your batting average, but it's going to take effort, homework, and making sure your inner circle for the fourth quarter is filled with family, friends, and advisors who can help you make better future decisions.

B.) *Some good, some bad.* (4 points)

Think about how you made the good decisions. Now think about what hindsight tells you were the causes of the bad decisions. Get your very best decision-maker (friend, family member, or advisor) to help you deconstruct your good and bad decisions. Fourth quarter success can come down to making a few more good decisions and fewer bad decisions. Perfection is unattainable: Sorry to all the type A personalities reading this who take this statement as a challenge!

C.) *Mostly good decisions.* (9 points)

Well done. Even Warren Buffet has trouble getting above 70% good decisions, but the key is he tries to make sure major decisions are examined more closely. The other challenge is to avoid paralysis by analysis and overthinking a major decision – a key art form for the fourth quarter.

2.) How would you describe your mental sharpness?

A.) *Not so good.* (0 points)

Let's figure out how to change this. Low mental

sharpness going into the fourth quarter can create
a lot of bad decision-making and fumbles.

B.) *I'm somewhat sharp, just need inspiration.* (4 points)
Let's figure out what your inspiration looks like. This shot
of mental energy will help you make better decisions
and engage better in the next chapter of your life.

C.) *I'm very sharp, on top of my game.* (9 points)
You should do well in the early stages of the fourth quarter.
Keeping that edge will be tough. You'll find that you are
even more disappointed deeper into the fourth quarter
if you lose that edge. Our brains tend to measure things
from what we think is normal for us; set the bar high and
disappointment can follow without regular mental workouts.
Even then, some loss of sharpness is normal as we age.

3.) Do you have family history of any form of dementia?

A.) *Yes.* (0 points)
This puts you at higher risk of losing mental acuity in the
fourth quarter, especially if the history is of early-onset
dementia. Rarely discussed is the damage done in the 3 to
5 years preceding diagnosis, when bad decisions may be
made before anyone realizes there is a problem in the brain
machinery. Pay attention to ways to catch the disease early
through cognitive tests and ways to slow down the disease.

B.) *No, but many of my family struggled with diminished
capacity later in life.* (3 points)
This may mean they lost their reason to get out of bed
in the morning, or it could mean chemical changes
in their brain. This is a good indicator that you need
to be even more mindful of keeping your mental
faculties sharp deep into the fourth quarter.

C.) *No history and my people stay fairly sharp almost to the end.* (8 points)
Great! A good family history is helpful and
gives you a leg up on staying sharp.

Having a Good Transition Plan

1.) How have you done in your life with major transitions?

A.) *Not so well.* (0 points)
Your ability to transition in prior experiences in your life gives
some clues as to how you'll do in the major fourth quarter
transition. Focus on chapter 4 and do extra homework,
including reading about and talking to been-there, done-
that people who have successfully transitioned from the
third quarter into the fourth quarter of their lives.

B.) *So-so.* (3 points)
You've had some good transitions and others didn't do well
at first or have always been a struggle. If you have an uneasy
feeling after reading chapter 4 and the fumbles highlighted,
take extra time to make sure the transition part gets done right.

C.) *Great.* (8 points)
Good for you! You will likely do fine with the fourth quarter
transitions, although keep in mind the stakes can feel
higher here than in other major transitions of your life.

**2.) Have you considered options for the next stage of your life
in the fourth quarter?**

A.) *Not much.* (3 points)
You're in the majority who give the next stage a little
thought now and again but think they can improvise as
they go and figure it out when they get there. Some can,
but most won't get the best plan going without more
homework and help from others in their network.

B.) *I've got some good ideas.* (6 points)
Better than no ideas. And one of the villains of decision

making, narrow framing (see chapter 3 on making better decisions), is best avoided by having a wider idea of options.

C.) *I've got many ideas and have already started exploring with family and friends which of these are best to start out with to fill a weekly calendar.* (9 points)

Congratulations, you're in the top 3% of people entering the fourth quarter. Exploring ideas for your next chapter of life intentionally and figuring out what options are good for your unique personality and circumstances make up the next step.

3.) How many of your family or friends have done well in fourth quarter transitions?

A.) *None.* (0 points)

This could be a problem. The nut doesn't fall too far from the tree. Without good examples and good mentors, getting your transition plan right will be challenging. Begin searching for others who have done well in their fourth quarter transition and spend time with them. Read stories of people you admire and see how they did it . . . or failed.

B.) *A few.* (4 points)

This is a good start. Now widen your network of fourth quarter success stories.

C.) *Quite a few friends and family have transitioned well into the fourth quarter.* (8 points)

Good, you are again part of the top 3% club of those who have a leg up in figuring out a good transition plan. Pivoting effectively as you enter different stages will also serve you well.

A Balanced Financial and Investment Strategy

1.) Do you have an up-to-date financial plan with carefully considered expenses and economic scenarios?

A.) *No plan, no clue what I should do.* (0 points)
Unless you have a nice income flow from a pension or family business, you may have many financial distractions early in the fourth quarter that prevent you from figuring out your *Why* in the next phase of your life.

B.) *I have a general game plan.* (4 points)
A general idea of your fourth quarter expenses, where cash flow will come from, and how to hedge inflation longer term is a very good start.

C.) *I have a well-thought-out, up-to-date plan.* (9 points)
Congratulations! Less than 3% of Americans have a written financial plan, and it's estimated less than 1% have a truly well-thought-out plan and keep it fresh going forward.

2.) How would you describe your financial margin of safety for the fourth quarter?

A.) *No margin of safety. Wal-Mart greeter may be in my future.* (0 points)
You're not alone. The Boston Center for Retirement Research estimates that 50% of Baby Boomers are in your situation. The options are few, with working longer into the fourth quarter at the top of the list. It's better to figure out how to use your unique talents to at least be able to work fewer hours deep into the fourth quarter rather than jobs that pay minimum wage.

B.) *Moderate margin of safety, have to be somewhat careful in spending and investing.* (4 points)
You've beat the odds of the average Baby Boomer. Now you need to keep better track of expenses going forward and be careful to not let fear or greed influence your fourth quarter investment decisions.

C.) *Wide margin of safety, will do fine in almost all scenarios.* (9 points)
Well done! Make sure you're protected from a perfect storm, a combination of unforeseen expenses, poor

investment decisions, and health-related problems. Or perhaps gray divorce. Now you can focus on the other 80% of fourth quarter decisions that lead to more happiness and fewer fumbles.

3.) Do you have a history of making bad investment decisions or poor spending choices based on short-term emotions like fear or greed?

A.) *Yes. I'm heavily influenced by friends and TV shows.* (0 points)
This is dangerous. You'll need to spend some time understanding the potential fumbles and doing additional study to improve your success ratio in the fourth quarter. A network of "make better decisions" friends (you may need to look for some new ones!) and a good professional financial advisor that you trust will also help.

B.) *I've only had a moderate number of problems in spending or investing along the way.* (4 points)
With an eye on your goals and some professional help (directly or through occasional surgical financial "second opinions"), you should be able to do better than average when it comes to fourth quarter spending and investing conundrums.

C.) *I've had very few bad decisions when it comes to spending or investing.* (9 points)
You are rare indeed! While the fourth quarter may throw you some curve balls that you didn't experience in the first three quarters, you should be better able to avoid these fumbles.

Having a Good Reason to Get Out of Bed

1.) Do you feel your unique talents and skills (your *Why*) are fully utilized today?

A.) *Not very well.* (0 points)
The MacArthur study found that having a purpose in life is critical to how well you age in the fourth quarter. Explore

what your *Why* could be. It could be something that seems small, such as helping Meals on Wheels provide food for shut-ins every week, but over time it can give you inner satisfaction and perhaps reinforce what you want to avoid in the fourth quarter; or it could become part of something bigger that will change the world for the better, a little or a lot. It could even be the role of the sage elder, working on ways to make your family stronger and more communal like families of yesteryear.

B.) *Moderately well.* (6 points)

This provides a good foundation for the future. To move towards wellness and away from absence of illness, consider how you can have a variety of activities that stretch your brain and allow you to communicate with a wide variety of interesting people.

C.) *Quite well. I bounce out of bed with a strong sense of purpose.*(10 points)

You will find many examples in this book of the role of purpose in helping us be successful in the fourth quarter. If you're still working, how will you keep your *Why* strong in the fourth quarter? Will it be an extension or small pivot off what you're doing today, or will it be something you've always wanted to do but didn't have the time? It might be both, the "genius of *and*" versus the "tyranny of *or.*"

Let me add a note of caution: Having a strong *Why* today doesn't always translate to a strong *Why* tomorrow.

2.) When someone asks you how you spend each day, do you light up with answers or shrug your shoulders and say, "Not much is happening"?

A.) *Mostly I say, "Not much is happening."* (0 points)

This is one of those warning signs. If you spend most of your time in the "Not much is happening" category, it won't end well. You might get so bored that you jump at the chance to be engaged when the first bright shiny object (a distraction) comes along. Experience tells me that chasing bright shiny objects is often a fourth quarter stress-relief mechanism that drives you farther way from a true *Why* and more towards possibly destructive activities to you or your family.

B.) *I have good days and bad days.* (6 points)
Good. You've created some longevity and wellness protection for the future. Consider making small steps towards having more good days and fewer bad days, the Kaizen concept discussed in chapter 3.

C.) *I light up almost all the time and love helping other people find their own Why.* (10 points)
Congratulations, you have checked off a very important box in the quest for wellness and happiness in the fourth quarter. Explore how helping other people find their *Why*, especially when they are struggling with other distractions like chronic pain or family problems, can benefit you.

3.) Is there a major life situation, such as a family or financial problem or you or a loved one having a chronic illness, distracting you and causing great anxiety?

A.) *Yes. It's hard to focus right now.* (2 points)
Another warning sign that finding your own *Why* may be more challenging. There are usually two choices in these situations: Either solve the problem (preferred but not always doable) or learn to adapt to a new normal, and build positives on top of other negatives.

B.) *We have several bubbling situations that could boil over in the near future.* (4 points)
Intervention before the crisis may be your near-term *Why*. You may need to marshal resources (people, experts, creative techniques) that are unfamiliar to you. As you widen the network of potential problem-solvers, be sure to bring others along for the brainstorming – or figure out ways to have others help.

C.) *Any small issues we have are being handled well by the individual and the family.* (9 points)

Great! The fourth quarter is full of unexpected twists and turns, plus those we know to expect. How you adjust to each situation, including when multiple challenges pile up, is a strong predictor of how well your overall fourth quarter will be and an indicator of how happy you've been along the way and will be at the end of life.

Wellness versus the Absence of Illness

1.) How much total time do you spend each day exercising or simply moving your body?

A.) *Less than an hour.* (2 points)

You're at higher risk of a host of diseases, including stroke, diabetes, osteoporosis, and even early dementia, with so little daily movement. Focus on the Wellness chapter and start with the Kaizen (small steps) concept.

B.) *One hour each day. I occasionally push myself to be fitter.* (9 points)

Good. Your activity level is a solid foundation for warding off illness. Taking it to the next level will help you move towards true wellness, which then leads to other benefits of fourth quarter engagement.

C.) *Two hours or more with a diverse workout program and frequent aerobic exercise. I push myself to be fit.* (20 points)

Great! You are in the top 3% of the aging population and have dramatically lowered your risk of many debilitating diseases. Since your ability to bounce back is so critical to fourth quarter happiness, make sure you have multiple exercise and movement options so you don't go from 3 hours of movement and exercise to 30 minutes a day as a result of an injury or illness.

2.) How well do you sleep?

A.) *Not very well.* (Minus 3 points)

This is very dangerous and puts you at risk for many fumbles, including depression and not having the energy to exercise or be engaged in life. In short, lack of sleep can lead to a complete fourth quarter collapse. Lack of exercise, caffeine, stress, worry, and many medical conditions (including chronic pain) can lead to poor sleep. So can distractions such as a snoring partner; consider ear plugs: Google "Mack's ear plugs" for easy purchasing options.

Harvard Health and the U.S. Dept. of Health and Human Services have guides to better sleep. Get one and determine how to improve your sleep deeper into the fourth quarter. You may need to consult your doctor and find a way to correct this before you begin experiencing a potentially catastrophic series of fumbles in the fourth quarter.

B.) *Pretty well. I get 4 to 6 hours of uninterrupted sleep every night.* (4 points)

Good. This is a reasonable foundation for warding off various ailments in the fourth quarter. It's not a great prescription for wellness and bouncing out of bed to seize the day. Harvard Health and the U.S. Dept. of Health and Human Services have guides to better sleep. Get one and determine how to improve your sleep deeper into the fourth quarter.

C.) *I get at least 6 to 8 hours of uninterrupted sleep every night.* (10 points)
Congratulations! You have a key asset to achieving wellness and happiness in the fourth quarter.

3.) Are you worried or angry a lot?

A.) *Yes. I worry or get upset frequently.* (0 points)

You are in the mainstream. As a result of the incessant bad-news drumbeat of the media machine, not to mention the well-meaning friends who share every disaster, big or small, happening around the world, our fight-or-flight primitive brain is more constantly on alert these days. Chronic worry can wear you and your immune system down.

If the source of worry or being upset is a spouse, life partner, or child (or grandchild), and good solutions to fix it aren't working or apparent, then you need to consider how you can best accept the situation with grace.

B.) *I usually worry or get upset once a day.* (3 points)
Good. This level of worry and getting upset occasionally can still create problems, but it's less likely to destroy your immune system and make you susceptible to a host of other problems. Although it's true that most things we worry about never happen, some of these emotions are baked into our DNA or the early scripts we learned when we were young from parents or other family members.

C.) *I rarely worry more than once or twice a week.* (10 points)
Congratulations! You have figured out how to maintain a more balanced demeanor in the face of challenges. This is a great skill set to have in the fourth quarter, but even more so given the unprecedented speed and level of change we are experiencing in our world today.

You probably figure out a solution to a problem, or if it can't be solved, you either accept it or concentrate on other more positive things in your life.

Social Networks Rule Even in the Fourth Quarter

1.) How many people did you have a good conversation (5 or more minutes) with today?

A.) *None.* (Minus 3 points)
This probably means you're living a relatively isolated life or not enjoying the company of family or friends around you. Or you've become engrossed with cable TV

or video games. You are at higher risk for depression and many diseases and for elder abuse. Getting more socially engaged may be critical to your fourth quarter success.

B.) *One or two.* (6 points)
This seems to be the norm for most people in the fourth quarter. You may be able to remain more disease-free at this level of engagement, but your chances of achieving true wellness are limited.

C.) *Three or more.* (10 points)
Congratulations! You are in the social wellness zone. Numerous studies suggest you have a lower risk of depression and many diseases, plus you have an active network that can help you rebound better if you develop mental – or physical-health problems.

2.) How would you describe your overall social network?

A.) *I have few friends and no intimate relationships.* (0 points)
Very dangerous to your health and sense of well-being. You are at high risk for becoming a hermit and developing depression and other diseases early in the fourth quarter.

B.) *I have a moderate number of friends, mostly old and dear friends.* (4 points)
Good, but as we enter the fourth quarter, it's inevitable that we start losing friends to illness or death, or they move too far away to maintain a good connection. Expand your list of new friends and make sure they are the kind of friends who make your day better, not remind you of all the problems in your life or in the world.

C.) *I have a number of friends, and I'm adding new, diverse friends to my network.* (9 points)
Great! It takes a mindful approach to tend your garden of friends, seeing less of those who add

stress to your life and adding new ones who help you look forward to every conversation.

3.) How much do you interact with children?

A.) *It's been many months, and I don't miss being around children.* (0 points)
Interaction with children is considered a fundamental requirement for humans to age well. Humans have been in close, communal families for thousands of years until recently. Find ways to interact meaningfully with children, whether it's your own grandchildren or volunteering for an elementary-school reading program.

B.) *It's been at least a week.* (4 points)
This means you have regular interactions, just not regular enough for true wellness. Even a phone call with a grandchild every week can maintain important social connections.

C.) *It's only been a few days, but I miss it.* (9 points)
Great! You're above the norm for our increasingly disconnected society. One fumble to avoid: As kids grow up, they get involved with numerous activities and it may be more difficult for you to stay engaged. Tend this garden as well and keep the curiosity and creativity of children ever-present deep into the fourth quarter.

Communicate Until the Cows Come Home

1.) How well can you apologize?

A.) *Not very well.* (0 points)
Most people have trouble saying they are sorry or accepting that they've been the source of a mistake or fumble. This can affect life partners; better hope they don't decide that gray divorce is less painful than living another 10 to 20 years or more with you. This can limit your number of

true friends and certainly strain family relations. Refer to chapter 9 for ideas on how to apologize better.

B.) *I'm average.* (4 points)
If you're really average, you may be above average for the population. Ask your life partner and a few friends how they would rate you on apologies and see if your self-assessment is accurate. By the way, if there's a disconnect between your assessment and those around you, consider there might be other disconnects between your perception of how people view you and how they really do.

C.) *I'm good at apologies.* (9 points)
Great! Spending more time with people around you in the fourth quarter may result in a test of your ability to apologize more frequently.

2.) How frequently do you say things that cause conversations to come to an abrupt end?

A.) *That happens a lot.* (Minus 3 points)
A dangerous warning sign that has implications for almost every chapter and fumble in this book. If you hold such strong opinions that others don't want to keep talking with you, you run many risks including gray divorce, depression, and isolation. Or you may fall into group think, where only people with your strong beliefs will hang around with you, creating a more limited ability to deal with many fumbles that lie ahead.

B.) *Occasionally that happens every week.* (2 points)
This may allow you to at least keep some friends in the fourth quarter, although it is unlikely you will achieve anything approaching true wellness with a robust relationships with friends and family.

C.) *This almost never happens.* (8 points)
Excellent! Being able to have a true conversation, without judging the other person, and listening respectfully puts you

in a good position to maintain good existing relationships and add some new ones in the fourth quarter.

3.) How would you rate your Emotional Intelligence (EQ), your ability to read people and adjust your communication style to the person and mood?

A.) *Not very highly.* (Minus 3 points)
This is an important area to focus on improving for the fourth quarter. EQ is a high predictor of success in many areas of life, and with all the challenges of the fourth quarter, it's an especially important skill to develop. The good news is it can be learned! See the basic elements of EQ in chapter 9.

B.) *Sometimes I do that well, but other times not so well.* (3 points)
This is a good foundation for the fourth quarter. Your current EQ skills can be sharpened in a variety of ways, including books on EQ, workshops, and webinars. See the basic elements of EQ in chapter 9.

C.) *I almost always read people well and adjust my communication with them accordingly.* (15 points)
Great! This gives you a strong ability to do well with relationships of many kinds in the fourth quarter. If for any reason you see this skill slipping, make great efforts to sharpen and maintain good EQ for as long as possible.

Thoughtful Estate Planning

1.) Do you have a well-thought-out estate plan?

A.) *Not really. I don't even have a will.* (0 points)
Dying intestate (without a will) is fraught with delays, costs, and the likelihood your estate won't be distributed the way you want it. See Dying Without a Will at: www.FourthQuartersFumbles.com.

B.) *Yes, although it hasn't been looked at in over 5 years and some things need to be changed.* (3 points)

Good timing for you to schedule a meeting with your estate attorney. Your financial planner can help you prepare for the meeting and provide guidelines for questions your attorney will ask.

C.) *Yes, and it's been updated within the last few years with good thought towards both the financial and nonfinancial aspects after I'm gone.* (7 points)
Well done! You have done what many, even the wealthy, don't do frequently enough. Kick the tires, make sure things are the way you want them and don't overthink avoiding estate and income taxes to the exclusion of other important estate considerations.

2.) Do you have good backup plans for how bills get paid and health decisions are made if your primary power of attorney isn't available?

A.) *No. Not sure who would do it.* (0 points)
This is dangerous even in a time where many regular bills can be on autopay. Ask your financial planner or estate attorney for options about naming a backup financial power of attorney and a health-care power of attorney.

B.) *Yes, although I have moderate concerns over the busy lives of my backups making it hard for them to handle this responsibility.* (3 points)
Many backups in powers of attorney are children who have multiple plates spinning with careers and families. Reconsider your options and ask your financial planner and estate attorney for alternatives to consider.

C.) *Yes, and I've valued common sense and have the right person in each backup role.* (7 points**)**
Great! You've likely avoided a potential fumble later in the fourth quarter.

3.) Have you avoided giving money to people or places you don't respect, and made sure inherited money will be used properly?

A.) *No. I just divided everything up equally and I'm hoping for the best.* (2 points)

An "old school" approach to estate planning. It sometimes works out fine but more often creates problems for heirs. Talk to your financial planner or estate attorney about options.

B.) *Yes. I've been thoughtful about money given to children versus community causes. I do wonder how some of my children will handle the money.* (5 points)

Good! You're ahead of many who do estate planning and you're asking the right questions. Make sure you're discussing this thoroughly with your life partner. He or she may have a different perspective on how much to give children versus community causes and how much is "enough" to give to children, and may have information you don't have that would influence how you pass assets at death.

C.) *Yes. I've been thoughtful about money given to children versus community causes. I've considered and balanced leaving money outright versus in trust to my family.* (8 points)

Great! You're in the top 1% when it comes to planning your estate.

Getting Your Living Options Right

1.) Do you like your plan for where you'll live as you age?

A.) *Don't really have a plan.* (0 points)

B.) You're in the majority. Most people don't seriously begin to think about housing options later in the fourth quarter until they are forced to by health problems or when they see friends developing problems staying in their own homes.

C.) *Have a general plan and think we may downsize, but not sure what we'll do after that.* (4 points)
Good. Having some kind of general plan is a good start. Doing more homework well before you need to make a decision is a good idea.

D.) *We have plans and have discussed options depending on our future health and finances.* (8 points)
Congratulations! You have reduced the potential for fumbles in this area. Recognize that you and your life partner may shift your opinions over time, especially as living options in your own home and in retirement communities become more diverse and modernized.

2.) Do you and your life partner agree on future housing options?

A.) *No. We're miles apart.* (Minus 3 points)
Dangerous! We've even seen one spouse stay in the family home and the other spouse move into a retirement community – not great for the marital relationship, possibly stressful on finances, family, and friend relationships.

B.) *Yes, although we're not set on location or exact timing.* (4 points)
Good! Over time, you can work on the where and the when, hopefully in advance of major changes in your health that may make you tear up your existing plan.

C.) *Yes, and we've narrowed down the where and when to a range of ages and circumstances in our lives, mostly depending on how our health holds up and our social network in the future.* (8 points)
Great! You've thought through various scenarios, which means you're more likely to pick up helpful bits of information along the way as you consider final decision-making downstream.

3.) Are you an introvert?

A.) *I need a lot of alone time, especially right after a big social interaction.* (3 points)

You are more likely to decide that your home is your sanctuary later in the fourth quarter and that you want to stay there no matter what. This may be fine as long as you can keep from becoming a hermit. Resist the urge to cocoon yourself more as you age. Being a true introvert can also cause numerous issues and potential fumbles if your life partner is more like (b) or (c) below.

B.) *I like my alone time but equally like socializing with friend and family.* (6 points)
Good. Your balance will likely mean you'll be able to make good decisions about your living arrangements through different fourth quarter stages.

C.) *I'm always eager to meet new people and engage with my friends and family.* (10 points)
Great! You will probably be fine wherever you live later in life. If life throws you unexpected problems that knock you off balance and make you want to withdraw in your home, try to find ways to get back to your curious outgoing self.

Cumulative Survey Results

180 Points or more

Congratulations! You're a fourth quarter model of success.

You have a much lower likelihood of experiencing major fourth quarter fumbles and a better chance than most people of bouncing back from the fumbles you do encounter. Your potential to achieve true wellness (and not just the absence of illness), leading to a great fourth quarter, is very high. Well done!

If your life partner has a much lower score, you're the designated leader. Even if you haven't had much success leading your life partner up to this point, get extra clever and creative in the fourth quarter and help him or her focus on strengths and compensate for weaknesses.

131-179 Points

You're well positioned for the fourth quarter.

You have a lower likelihood of fumbles than most people. You are on track to having a good fourth quarter, but to get to great is going to take some intentional thought, homework, and action. You have a few fumble areas that you want to study to make sure you at least now what may throw you off course.

80-130 Points

Build on your strengths and shore up your weaknesses.

You're doing well in some areas and not so well in others. This is a good wake-up call to get better prepared for the fourth quarter. It's never too late to adapt positive changes that can help you avoid fumbles and move towards more true happiness in the years to come.

Below 80 Points

You may have a rough road ahead. It's time for action!

The good news is you now know in advance that you have a high likelihood of experiencing fumbles in the fourth quarter. This is better than looking backward many years from now with many regrets and wondering how your life could have been different. Focus on ways you can improve your *How Much?*, your *How?*, your *Why?*, your *Who?* and your *Where?* Now, what are you going to do about it?

APPENDIX 2:

Index of Potential Red-Zone Fumbles

Making Better Decisions

Having a Good Transition Plan

A Balanced Financial and Investment Plan

Having a Good Reason to Get Out of Bed

Wellness versus the Absence of Illness

APPENDIX 3:

Values Assessment

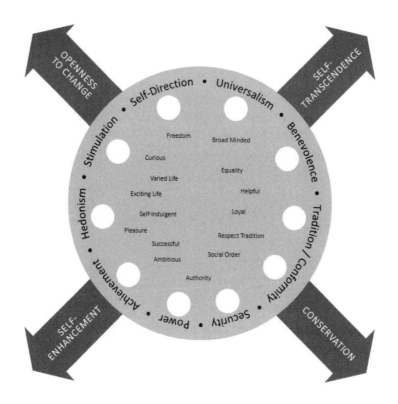

Put a 1, 2 or 3 in each blank circle – if the words on the outer ring and inside the circle are a lot like you, put a 3. If they are somewhat like you, put a 2. If they are a little like you, put a 1. If they are nothing like you, leave it blank. When you're finished, place a plus sign (+) on each side where you have the highest scores and a minus sign (-) on the side(s) where you have the lowest scores.

Most of us have a dominant side or two. Knowing your dominant side helps as you work on keeping fourth quarter activities aligned with your core values.

APPENDIX 4:

Mapping Your Time in the Fourth Quarter

Spending Your Time	**The Ideal Week in Retirement**		
	Morning	**Afternoon**	**Evening**
SUNDAY			
MONDAY			
TUESDAY			
WEDNESDAY			
THURSDAY			
FRIDAY			
SATURDAY			

"Your most valuable asset is time, not money. A rich life is about spending that time well." — Mitch Anthony

APPENDIX 5:

Resources, Notes, and References

CHAPTER 1:

Why So Many Seniors Fumble the Ball in the Fourth Quarter

Favorite books:

» *Another Country: Navigating the Emotional Terrain of our Elders* by Mary Pipher is an excellent book delving into the challenges that seniors face, including the loss of community.

» *Age Wave* by Dr. Ken Dychtwald, one of the foremost thought leaders on population aging and its profound business, social, financial, health-care, workforce, and cultural implications. www.agewave.com

Other resources:

• **EBRI Retirement studies: https://www. ebri.org/surveys/rcs/2016/**

• **The MacArthur Study of Successful Aging was initiated in 1988 to study factors associated with "successful aging"** – that is, living longer while avoiding major cognitive and physical disability. Participants were recruited on the basis of age (70 to 79 years only) and physical and cognitive functioning from three communities in the eastern United States: Durham, North Carolina; East Boston, Massachusetts; and New Haven, Connecticut. More than 4,000 age-eligible men and women were screened using four criteria of physical functioning and two criteria of cognitive functioning to identify those functioning in the top third of the age group.

- **The MacArthur Research Network on an Aging Society was created in 2008 with a $3.9 million grant from the Foundation.** The Network's founding chair, Dr. John Rowe, is the former CEO of Aetna and a professor at the Columbia University Mailman School of Public Health. Previously, Dr. Rowe led the groundbreaking MacArthur Research Network on Successful Aging, which helped change America's concept of aging from a period of inevitable decline to a more nuanced and positive view of life beyond 60 and published the best-selling book *Successful Aging*.

- **Cleveland Clinic study on patient movement:** http://www. npr.org/sections/health-shots/2015/07/06/419519145/people-with-brain-injuries-heal-faster-if-they-get-up-and-get-moving

CHAPTER 2:

Keys to Fourth Quarter Happiness

Favorite books:

» *No Ordinary Disruption: The Four Global Forces Breaking All the Trends* by Richards Dobbs, James Manyika, and Jonathan Woetzel (the McKinsey team referenced in the book) – helps understanding of the high level of change happening in the world today.

» *Thank You for Being Late: An Optimists Guide to Thriving in the Age of Accelerations* by Thomas L. Friedman, a wide-ranging view of today's fast-paced change, what it may mean for our society, and how to deal with it.

» *The Gift of Years: Growing Old Gracefully* by Joan Chittister. A celebrated spiritual writer, Joan looks at the many dimensions of the fourth quarter from a different perspective than most thought leaders. "These are the capstone years, the time in which a whole new life is in the making again."

Other resources:

- **INSERM study of half a million French citizens who delayed retirement:** http://www. nbcnews.com/health/delaying-retirement-can-delay-dementia-large-study-finds-6C10637029

- **Smartphones are accessed an average of 80 – 150 times per day by the typical user.** The negative effects on our sense of well-being, and heightened anxiety, are now being recognized: https://www.wsj.com/articles/ how-smartphones-hijack-our-minds-1507307811

- *Wall Street Journal* **article on why bucket-list obsessions can hurt fourth quarter happiness:** https://www.wsj.com/articles/ its-time-to-rethink-the-bucket-list-retirement-1458525877

- **Merrill Lynch 2016 Leisure in Retirement: Beyond the Bucket List study:** https://agewave. com/wp-content/uploads/2016/05/2016-Leisure-in-Retirement_Beyond-the-Bucket-List.pdf

- **Early detection of dementia?** *Journal of Biophotonics*, March 2016, Vol. 9. Iss. 3, "An Infrared Sensor Analysing Label-Free the Secondary Structure of the Abeta Peptide in Presence of Complex Fluids," by Andreas Nabers, et al.

Chapter 3:

Making Better Decisions

Favorite books:

» *Thinking Fast and Slow*, by Nobel Economics prize winner Daniel Kahneman. There are numerous examples in this book of how the "fast brain," the one that handles everyday tasks quickly and efficiently, is used too often to answer questions when the "slow brain" should have been engaged. This seems to occur much too often in the fourth quarter!

» *9 Things You Simply Must Do to Succeed in Love and Life: A Psychologist Learns from His Patients What Really Works and What Doesn't* by Dr. Henry Cloud. These nine things are great to post in a prominent place in your home office or on the refrigerator, perhaps a subtle reminder to your life partner?

» *Decisive: How to Make Better Choices in Life and Work* by Chip and Dan Heath. A great read and a good book to promote better decision making to give to your children, grandchildren, and friends.

» *Your Money and Your Brain: How the New Science of Neuroeconomics Can Help Make You Rich,* Jason Zweig does an in-depth look at what actually goes on inside our brains when we make decisions about money.

» *Hardiness: Turning Stressful Circumstances into Resilient Growth* by Salvatore R. Maddi is a book that discusses decades of research, defining the special value of hardiness: being resilient by not only surviving but thriving under stress, thereby achieving happiness and fulfillment in living. The book includes "hardiness assessment and training."

» *Finding Flow: The Psychology of Engagement with Everyday Life* by Mihaly Csikszentmihalyi. A lot of good ideas on finding flow, a state of positive fulfillment, in the fourth quarter.

» *The Resilience Factor: 7 Keys to Finding Your Inner Strength and Overcoming Life's Hurdles* by Karen Reivich and Andrew Shatte has many good ideas on how to overcome adversity to become a happy, well-adjusted person. "Resilience transforms. It transforms hardship into challenge, failure into success, helplessness into power"

» "Everything can be taken from a man but one thing: the last of the human freedoms – to choose one's attitude in any given set of circumstances, to choose one's own way." This is a quotation from Viktor E. Frankl's *Man's Search for Meaning*.

Few books of the last century have had a greater impact on our quest for meaning than this book. It's an all-time bestseller by a Jewish man who had just lost everything in the Holocaust. When Frankl, emaciated from concentration camps, returned to his beloved Vienna, no one was there to meet him. His mother had been gassed at Auschwitz. His brother had been killed in another camp. His wife, Tilly, had starved to death in the women's camp at Bergen-Bergen. Now, he wondered, what was the point of his life?

Other resources:

- **What highly successfully aging nuns tell us about memory:** http://memory.foundation/2014/12/01/what-nuns-show-us-about-memory/

- **Fear of Success:** http://scholarworks.waldenu.edu/cgi/viewcontent.cgi?article=1878&context=dissertations

- **Resiliency and loss for children and adults.** Create circles of like-minded people who understand what you're going through. **http://www.experience.camp/**

- **Growth versus fixed mind-set: a high predictor of avoiding fumbles in the fourth quarter.** http://jamesclear.com/fixed-mindset-vs-growth-mindset

- **A YouTube video on growth versus fixed mind-sets** for those who do better watching than reading. **https://www.youtube.com/watch?v=KUWn_TJTrnU**

CHAPTER 4:

Having a Good Transition Plan

Favorite books:

- » *Option B: Facing Adversity, Building Resilience, and Finding Joy* by Sheryl Sandberg and Adam Grant, has great stories about how to bounce back after the death of a life partner. Sheryl lost her husband Dave too early. Check out the Option B community at www.facebook.com/OptionBOrg

» *Gray Divorce, Silver Linings* by Haleh Moddasser, CPA, is an SFG Field Guide to navigating later stage divorce. Going through the trauma of separating from a long-time in the fourth quarter? Well written and researched, this is a primer on dealing with this new, fast-growing challenge.

» *Transitions: Making the Most of Life's Changes* is a classic book by William Bridges. Considered by many to be a definitive work on transition planning.

» *Ring in the Rubble* by Dr. Gary Bradt is a thought provoking book helping us understand how we can find silver linings despite setbacks in life.

» *The Best Seat in the House: How I Woke up One Tuesday and was Paralyzed for Life* by Allen Rucker. This is another thought-provoking book, the very personal, and occasionally funny account by a man who was suddenly rendered a paraplegic by a rare health condition. He describes how his abruptly changed circumstances forced him to reevaluate his life.

» *The Grief Recovery Handbook* by John James and Russell Friedman is a good guide that has helped many of our clients and friends.

Other resources:

• **Modern Widows Club**: Chapters around the country create the "circles" concept that help with bouncing back from adversity. Look for good chemistry but be open to new experience and give it time to determine if a particular circle is right for you.

• Soren Kierkegaard said, **"Life can only be understood backwards; but it must be lived forwards."** There is no perfect transition or financial plan. The key is in the planning process and the ability to pivot when needed.

CHAPTER 5:

A Balanced Financial and Investment Strategy

Favorite books:

» *The Intelligent Investor* by Benjamin Graham, updated version by Jason Zweig. Warren Buffet calls this "By far the best book on investing ever written." Considered the value investor's foundation for decision making.

» *The Millionaire Next Door* by Danko and Stanley. Acquiring and keeping wealth in America is more often the result of hard work, diligent savings, and living below your means than it is about inheritance, advance degrees, and even intelligence.

» *Worth It: Your Life, Your Money, Your Terms* by Amanda Steinberg. The CEO of dailyworth. com reframes money's meaning in your life.

» *The 100-Year Life: Living and Working in an Age of Longevity* by Lynda Gratton and Andrew Scott, professors from the London Business School. Focused on how to financially save for a longer life, this book is much more. It provides some interesting analysis, exciting predictions and straightforward recommendations.

Other resources:

• **Nineteen questions to ask your financial advisor** to make sure they are working in your best interest from the Wall Street Journal's Jason Zweig: http://jasonzweig. com/the-19-questions-to-ask-your-financial-adviser/

CHAPTER 6:

Having a Good Reason to Get Out of Bed

Favorite books:

» *Halftime: Changing Your Game Plan from Success to Significance* by Bob Bufford. A classic for men who have lost their true north perspective.

» *On Purpose Person: Making Your Life Make Sense* by Kevin McCarthy. Discover and define your life purpose, your "true north."

» *MOJO: How to Get It, How to Keep It, How to Get It Back if You Lose It* by Marshall Goldsmith. One of the premier life coaches profiles best practices in living a life you will be proud of.

» *Encore: Finding Work that Matters in the Second Half of Life* by Marc Freedman has many good concepts that relate to fourth quarter planning, especially if you're behind the curve in financial planning and need good extra income to balance your wants and needs.

» *The Encore Career Handbook: How to Make a Living and a Difference in the Second Half of Life* by Marci Alboher provides lots of good ideas for the fusion of doing well while doing good for the world.

Other resources:

• Harvard health study: http://www.health.harvard.edu/blog/ is-retirement-good-for-health-or-bad-for-it-201212105625

• Website for exploring activities in the next chapter of your life: www.encore.org

CHAPTER 7:

Wellness versus the Absence of Illness

Favorite books:

» ***Younger Next Year: Live Strong, Fit, and Sexy – Until You're 80 and Beyond*** by Chris Crowley and Henry is a classic book on how to stay mentally, physically, and spiritually fit deep into the fourth quarter.

» ***Why it Hurts: A Physician's Insights on The Purpose of Pain*** by Dr. Aneesh Singla. She is a Harvard-trained physician and pain management specialist, answering questions in his book like why we actually feel pain, along with what its purpose might be. Here are a few things you may gain from reading *Why It Hurts:*

- Professional Physician Insight
- A Historical Journey through Medicine and Pain Killers
- Understanding About Opioids
- A New Perspective on Pain
- Greater Awareness for Your Body
- New Thoughts of Chronic pain and the "Need to Cure"

» ***Mistreated: Why We Think We're Getting Good Health Care – and Why We're Usually Wrong*** by Robert Pearl. An interesting book written as a testament to Pearl's father who was misdiagnosed and died after surviving all manner of challenges. He profiles how the U.S. spends 50% more on healthcare than any other nation in the world, yet our outcomes on almost every measure of quality are in the bottom half of industrialized countries. According to a recent study from Johns Hopkins, medical errors, including hospital-acquired infections, medication mistakes and poor communication among clinicians, contribute to 251,000 deaths a year.

» ***Slow Medicine: The Way to Healing*** by Victoria Sweet. An accomplished physician, Sweet describes the changing craft and art, as well as science, of medicine. Sweet believes through her hard-earned wisdom that no algorithm can replace the human touch that brings together "fast" and "slow" in a truly effective, efficient, sustainable, and humane way of healing.

» *You Bet Your Life: The 10 Mistakes Every Patient Makes* by Trisha Torrey is an eye-opening look at fumbles that occur navigating the health-care system.

» *You Staying Young* by Roizen and Oz. A wide array of practical advice from prominent doctors on health and wellness.

» *The Body Builders: Inside the Science of the Engineered Human* by Adam Piore. This book combines vivid storytelling with groundbreaking science to give you a glimpse into what the future may hold from medical science for repairing our bodies.

» *Aging and the Digital Life Course* is a collection of essays edited by David Prendergast and Chiara Garattini, anthropologists at Intel. A candid look at how technology can and is being used in our aging society.

» *The Emotional Survival Guide for Caregivers* by Dr. Barry Jacobs. A great read if you're a caregiver for an aging family member and want to know how to better deal with the many issues you'll face.

Other resources:

- **Higher midlife fitness can impact brain health in later life** (Annals of Internal Medicine 2013): https://www.cooperinstitute.org/pub/news.cfm?id=143

- **When It Comes to Longevity, Regular Exercise May Be the Most Potent Weapon Against Disease (Wall Street Journal Online 2010):** https://www.cooperinstitute.org/pub/news.cfm?id=70

- The Cooper Institute Finds High Midlife Fitness and Cardiovascular Health Associated With Lower Healthcare Costs (Journal of the American College of Cardiology **and American Journal of Preventive Medicine** 2015): https://www.cooperinstitute.org/pub/news.cfm?id=175

- New Study Shows Higher Midlife Fitness is Key to Healthier Aging (The Archives of Internal Medicine 2012): *https://www.cooperinstitute.org/pub/news.cfm?id=134*

- Centers for Disease Control and Prevention: www.cdc.gov

- Cooper Clinic: http://www.cooperaerobics.com/ Ken Cooper's 8 steps to wellness include many of the cautions and prescriptions included in this book.

- Majority of doctors performing delicate procedures don't have strong experience: http://www.nytimes.com/2003/02/10/nyregion/study-finds-many-doctors-performing-surgery-lack-practice-with-procedures.html

- Mayo Clinic: www.mayo.edu

- The Qualcomm challenge to create a Star Trek tricorder, an advanced diagnostic device: https://tricorder.xprize.org/

- European Society of Cardiology study: https://www.escardio.org/The-ESC/Press-Office/Press-releases/moderate-physical-activity-linked-with-50-reduction-in-cardiovascular-death-in

- Dangers of too much sitting: https://www.livescience.com/55570-sitting-risks-exercise.html

- Benefits of walking for peripheral artery disease: *Journal of Vascular Surgery*: http://www.jvascsurg.org/article/S0741-5214(13)01585-1/pdf

- Fewer colds and walking: http://www.npr.org/templates/story/story.ph

- Brain benefits from 20 minutes of walking (University of Illinois study)

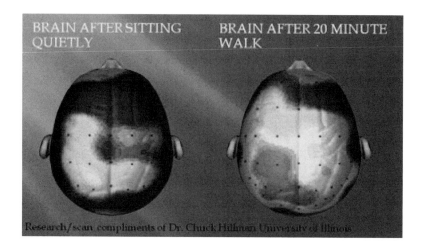

BRAIN AFTER SITTING QUIETLY

BRAIN AFTER 20 MINUTE WALK

Research/scan compliments of Dr. Chuck Hillman University of Illinois

The above image shows the brain activity before and after a 20-minute walk. The areas that "light up" are associated with happiness and good mental health.

- **Being a better health-care advocate (From Johns Hopkins):**

  Today, whether it's the nurse, social worker, patient liaison, or service-excellence coordinator, advocates round out the complete care package to help patients receive the best care realistically possible. Below are 10 skill sets that help health-care advocates provide services to their patients.

- ***Communicating:*** Health-care advocates educate patients and their families by interfacing with providers and payers to ensure patients understand their diagnoses, prognoses, treatment options, and post-treatment instructions.

- ***Promoting patient safety, empowerment, and rights:*** Advocates educate patients about their rights within the health-care system, safety, procedures and treatments, discharge instructions, costs, and insurance coverage. Health-care advocates are tasked with presenting this information in a transparent and meaningful way to help the patient fully understand their choices. This responsibility is a key component of being an advocate.

- *A working knowledge of medical terminology and the health-care system:* Understanding the complex nature of health-care requires attention to detail and an excellent grasp of medical terminology. Appropriate and thorough notation and documentation of issues expressed by patients regarding their care is essential. Fully understanding a patient's preferences and goals and being able to communicate them to providers is also important.

- *Understanding cost options in health care:* A key responsibility of a health-care advocate is helping patients navigate the stressful financial aspects of health care. This includes educating patients on reimbursement, billing, and financing options. Advocates also have extensive knowledge of insurance plans and their coverage options and limitations.

- *Resolution and follow up:* Through active listening, health-care advocates find solutions to patient concerns and bring issues to the attention of providers and payers. This is especially important for patients with chronic health conditions or complex medical needs where care may need to be coordinated among multiple providers. Advocates work closely with both the patient and providers to ensure the patient continues to receive the best care and outcomes realistically possible.

- *Professionalism in maintaining and ensuring patient confidence:* Patient advocates understand the legal and ethical issues surrounding private health information. They operate at a high level of discretion regarding patient and family information, complaints, issues, and regulatory compliance. It is very important that health-care advocates are trustworthy and have high ethical standards so they are trusted liaisons among patients, caregivers, and health-care professionals, which leads to better and safer care.

- *Being proactive:* Health-care advocates may work as patient-care coordinators ensuring all providers are informed about treatments, tests, and medications. In some instances, they may be able to review the patient's health records for accuracy and take necessary action to resolve any issues and quickly address patient concerns.

- *Improving systems and policy:* A hospital advocate works to decrease risk to the hospital by ensuring that patients' complaints and grievances are reported and acted upon in a timely manner – and that the hospital takes steps to prevent reoccurrence in the future. Patient advocates who enter into a policy career may also help to develop policies to improve systems, reduce overall health-care costs, and positively affect patient safety and outcomes.

- *Relationship building:* Health-care advocates may have clinical or administrative backgrounds in the health-care system (e.g., former case managers, doctors, nurses) and can use their experiences to help patients navigate the bureaucracy of this complex environment. The patient advocate works to create trusting relationships between patients and providers, which helps to reduce anxiety and fear and improve outcomes. They are vital members of the community and serve to empower patients.

- *Professional development:* There is currently no certification or credentialing for patient advocacy in the U.S. However, there are ethical guidelines and parameters promoted by professional organizations such as the National Patient Advocate Foundation to drive industry standards, educate patients and health-care workers, and partner with other state and federal organizations.

- *The journal of nutrition, health and aging,* December 2016, Vol. 20, Iss. 10. **"Tea Consumption Reduces the Incidence of Neurocognitive Disorders: Findings from the Singapore Longitudinal Aging Study,"** by L. Feng, et al.

CHAPTER 8:

Social Networks Rule Even in the Fourth Quarter

Favorite books:

> » Mary C. Morrison, author of *Let Evening Come: Reflections on Aging*, has many good views on navigating social networks we're not familiar with as we age and how to "go with the flow" of aging.

> » *Me, Myself, and Us: The Science of Personality and the Art of Well-Being* by Brian R. Little can help with developing a social network, with many resources you can call upon when you need them in the fourth quarter.

Other resources:

- "Social Capital and Community Resilience" by Daniel P. Aldrich and Michelle A. Meyer in *American Behavioral Scientist*, volume 59 (2015), pages 254-269. **How does your community stack up on the five essential elements that predict the ability to bounce back from disaster? http://theconversation. com/recovering-from-disasters-social-networks-matter-more-than-bottled-water-and-batteries-69611**

CHAPTER 9:

Communicate Until the Cows Come Home

Favorite books:

> » Martin Seligman's marvelous book, *Learned Optimism: How to Change Your Mind and Your Life*. A great primer for avoiding fourth quarter fumbles.

> » *When Sorry Isn't Enough: Making Things Right With Those You Love* by Gary Chapman and Jennifer Thomas is an excellent

look into the five ways we want to get apologies and the ways people give them (if they do), which don't always line up. Jen Thomas also did a TEDx talk, *"Getting the Last Word in Apology."*

» *How to Say it to Seniors: Closing the Communication Gap* by David Solie, one of the finest books on children communicating better with elders, also has many good ideas if you're the elder trying to understand and communicate with other elders around you.

» *Fierce Conversations: Achieving Success at Work and in Life One Conversation at a Time* by Susan Scott. If you're an introvert, this book can give you some ideas on how to have better discussions with people who naturally have the gift of gab.

» Norman Vincent Peale's classic book, *The Power of Positive Thinking*, deserves another look in the fourth quarter.

» Afraid that the new Roman Empire (America) is in Decline? *The Rational Optimist* by Matt Ridley highlights how much progress the world has made.

Other resources:

• **How good are you at admitting mistakes?** "Learning from Mistakes is Easier Said than Done: Group and Organizational Influences on the Detection and Correction of Human Error" by Amy C. Edmondson in *The Journal of Applied Behavioral Science,* volume 32 (1996), pages 5-28.

CHAPTER 10:

Thoughtful Estate Planning

Favorite books:

» *The Wall Street Journal Complete Estate-Planning Guidebook* by Rachel Emma Silverman. This book walks you step-by-step through the estate-planning process. It has solid advice on how to get the most out of the main estate planning tools, including wills, trusts, life insurance, guardianship papers, and powers-of-attorney documents.

This book will help you:

- Clarify your estate-planning goals, such as dividing up property for heirs, reducing taxes, or leaving money for charity.

- Understand the key estate-planning documents you'll need, including wills, beneficiary-designation forms, powers-of-attorney, and health-care advance directives.

- Decode the technical jargon that estate planners often use, so you feel comfortable discussing QTIPs and QPRTs when you sit down with your lawyer.

- Reduce possible estate, gift, or generation-skipping taxes and legal and probate fees, decreasing what goes to the tax man and increasing what goes to your heirs.

- Learn strategies to divide money and personal property among your heirs and reduce the possibility of family fights.

- Discuss sensitive estate-planning issues with your family.

- Maintain your estate-plan over time, including how to store and when to update your documents.

Other resources:

- **Percentage of Americans without a will:** https://www.forbes.com/sites/kateashford/2016/06/30/no-will/#6fea13ca2f20

CHAPTER 11:

Getting Your Living Options Right

Favorite books:

> » *Aging in the Right Place* by Golant argues that that the aging-in-place (staying in your home) idea has been oversold,

particularly by home health-care providers, builders eager to capitalize on renovating homes for older people, and financial institutions who have popularized reverse mortgages.

» *How to Age in Place: Planning for a Happy, Independent, and Financially Secure Retirement* by Dr. Mary Languirand. Clinical psychologists and aging specialists Mary Languirand and Robert Bornstein promote aging with dignity and comfort in the place of their own choosing. Features useful, actionable advice on making your home physically safe; getting around; obtaining necessary services; keeping a healthy mind, body, and spirit; and post-retirement employment.

» *Find the Right CCRC for Yourself or a Loved One* by Ruth Alvarez. One study revealed 60% of new residents made their *Where?* decision based on the Continuing Care Retirement Community's (CCRC) own marketing materials. Yet, only 11 states require review of those materials. This book covers the types of housing and contracts, entrance and monthly fees, essential things every CCRC should have, what guarantees you'll get, and what to do if things don't work out the way you hoped. Learn how to get family members to move into a CCRC, what to look for when you tour assisted living and nursing facilities, and what accreditations and certifications are important and which aren't.

» *Where Should I Live When I Retire?: A Guide to Continuing-Care Communities* by Bernice Hunt. This book explains what CCRCs are, how they operate, and what they offer. You'll learn what to look for, what to steer clear of, what you have a right to expect, and how you can best make the transition when you move.

» *Stages of Senior Care* by Paula and Lori Hogan. The founders of senior care giant Home Instead discuss the stages of later stage aging and the decision to age at-home.

» *Navigating the Journey of Aging Parents* by Cheryl Kuba. One of the few books I've read that addresses the fourth quarter almost exclusively from the perspective of the care recipient.

Other resources:

- A blog that gives you many perspectives on living options and avoiding fumbles later in life: http://www.aplaceformom.com/blog/social-life-for-seniors-why-assisted-living-is-better/

- Unconventional living options, including shipboard and shared living spaces: https://bethanylutheranvillage.org/blog/5-unconventional-retirement-living-options/

- Cost of long term care in your area: https://www.genworth.com/about-us/industry-expertise/cost-of-care.html

APPENDIX 6:

Fourth Quarter Fumbles Wheel Exercise

Directions: This exercise will assist you to evaluate where you are on the playing field in relation to each of these fourth quarter focus areas. Once completed, it will give you a visual of how well-rounded your life is as well as allow you to measure the success of that focus area.

> **Step 1** – Place a dot on each spoke indicating where you feel you are in regard to that particular focus area, using the 1-10 scale, with 1 being a low score and 10 being the best score.
>
> **Step 2** – Now, connect the dots to see how your balance wheel turns out.
>
> **Step 3** – Is your balance wheel-rounded? Are there flat spots on your wheel? Are you seeing areas that might need a little attention? What can you do to score each focus area higher, resulting in a more well-rounded balance wheel?

Your Own Life Balance Wheel

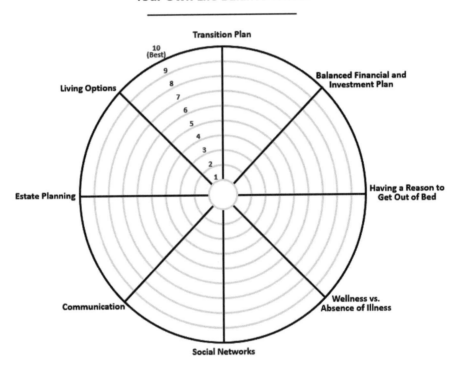

APPENDIX 7:

Holmes-Rahe Life Stress Inventory

The Holmes-Rahe Life Stress Inventory
The Social Readjustment Rating Scale
INSTRUCTIONS: Mark down the point value of each of these life events that has happened to you during the previous year. Total these associated points.

Life Event	Mean Value
1. Death of spouse	100
2. Divorce	73
3. Marital Separation from mate	65
4. Detention in jail or other institution	63
5. Death of a close family member	63
6. Major personal injury or illness	53
7. Marriage	50
8. Being fired at work	47
9. Marital reconciliation with mate	45
10. Retirement from work	45
11. Major change in the health or behavior of a family member	44
12. Pregnancy	40
13. Sexual Difficulties	39
14. Gaining a new family member (i.e.. birth, adoption, older adult moving in, etc)	39
15. Major business readjustment	39
16. Major change in financial state (i.e.. a lot worse or better off than usual)	38
17. Death of a close friend	37
18. Changing to a different line of work	36
19. Major change in the number of arguments w/spouse (i.e.. either a lot more or a lot less than usual regarding child rearing, personal habits, etc.)	35
20. Taking on a mortgage (for home, business, etc..)	31
21. Foreclosure on a mortgage or loan	30
22. Major change in responsibilities at work (i.e. promotion, demotion, etc.)	29
23. Son or daughter leaving home (marriage, attending college, joined mil.)	29
24. In-law troubles	29
25. Outstanding personal achievement	28
26. Spouse beginning or ceasing work outside the home	26
27. Beginning or ceasing formal schooling	26
28. Major change in living condition (new home, remodeling, deterioration of neighborhood or home etc.)	25
29. Revision of personal habits (dress manners, associations, quitting smoking)	24
30. Troubles with the boss	23
31. Major changes in working hours or conditions	20
32. Changes in residence	20
33. Changing to a new school	20
34. Major change in usual type and/or amount of recreation	19
35. Major change in church activity (i.e.. a lot more or less than usual)	19
36. Major change in social activities (clubs, movies,visiting, etc.)	18
37. Taking on a loan (car, tv,freezer,etc)	17
38. Major change in sleeping habits (a lot more or a lot less than usual)	16
39. Major change in number of family get-togethers ("")	15
40. Major change in eating habits (a lot more or less food intake, or very different meal hours or surroundings)	15
41. Vacation	13
42. Major holidays	12
43. Minor violations of the law (traffic tickets, jaywalking, disturbing the peace, etc)	11

Now, add up all the points you have to find your score.

150pts or less means a relatively low amount of life change and a low susceptibility to stress-induced health breakdown.

150 to 300 pts implies about a 50% chance of a major health breakdown in the next 2 years.

300pts or more raises the odds to about 80%, according to the Holmes-Rahe statistical prediction model.

About the Author

Dennis Stearns, CFP®, Stearns Financial Group

Dennis Stearns is an award-winning financial planner, futurist, entrepreneur, community leader, author, TEDx speaker, and the president of Stearns Financial Group, a fee-only investment management, financial, and business-planning firm with offices in Chapel Hill and Greensboro, North Carolina.

Dennis regularly leads best-practice workshops and delivers keynote presentations on investing and financial planning at local, regional, and national conferences. He was selected to be the facilitator at a major think tank in Boston for the leaders of the aging movement, including representatives from Social Security, Medicare, AARP, the Boston Center for Retirement Research, National Endowment for Financial Education, and many others.

He has been named "one of the leading financial scenario experts and futurists" by the Financial Planning Association.

Dennis is the author of several books, including *CEO Road Rules: Right Focus, Right People, Right Execution. Road Rules* was praised by Good to Great level-5 leader Daniel Jordt, former CEO of Walgreens.

Stearns Financial is the only financial firm in the Triad area of North Carolina to be named four consecutive years to the Financial Times "Top 300 financial firms" list.

In 2016, Dennis was named one of the *Triad Business Journal's* "Most Admired CEOs" and has also been named to the "Triad's Most Influential People" list.

He is an advisory board member for the Chamber Entrepreneur Launch program, a partner in a technology business accelerator and is treasurer and a board member for the Gateway University Research Park.

An active community leader, Dennis has earned two national Community Service Awards.

Dennis is a former chess expert and member of one of the winningest Pan-American chess teams in U.S. history. Today he coaches an inner-city chess club and plays chess with up to 30 people at the same time to raise money for children's charities.